CANADA
Activity and Fact Book

Canadian Geography Workbook for Kids

Capitals, Flags, Mammals, Birds, Fish, Trees, Flowers, Cities, Interesting Facts

Published by Dylanna Press an imprint of Dylanna Publishing, Inc.
Copyright © 2022 by Dylanna Press

Editor: Julie Grady

All rights reserved. No part of this publication may be reproduced, stored in a retrieval system, or transmitted by any means, including electronic, mechanical, photocopying, or otherwise, without prior written permission of the publisher.

Limit of liability/Disclaimer of Warranty: The Publisher and the author make no representations or warranties with respect to the accuracy or completeness of the contents of this work and specifically disclaim all warranties, including without limitation warranties of fitness for a particular purpose.

Although the publisher has taken all reasonable care in the preparation of this book, we make no warranty about the accuracy or completeness of its content and, to the maximum extent permitted, disclaim all liability arising from its use.

Trademarks: Dylanna Press is a registered trademark of Dylanna Publishing, Inc. and may not be used without written permission.
info@dylannapubishing.com

Color the Provinces

Color the provinces and territories and then use the map to answer the questions below.

1. Which are the only two landlocked provinces? _____
2. Which is the northernmost province? _____
3. Which is the southernmost province? _____
4. Which is the westernmost province? _____
5. Which provinces/territories border Alberta? _____
6. Which is the only province that is an island? _____
7. Which is the easternmost province? _____
8. Which provinces/territories share a border with the United States?_____

Alberta

Motto: *Strong and Free*

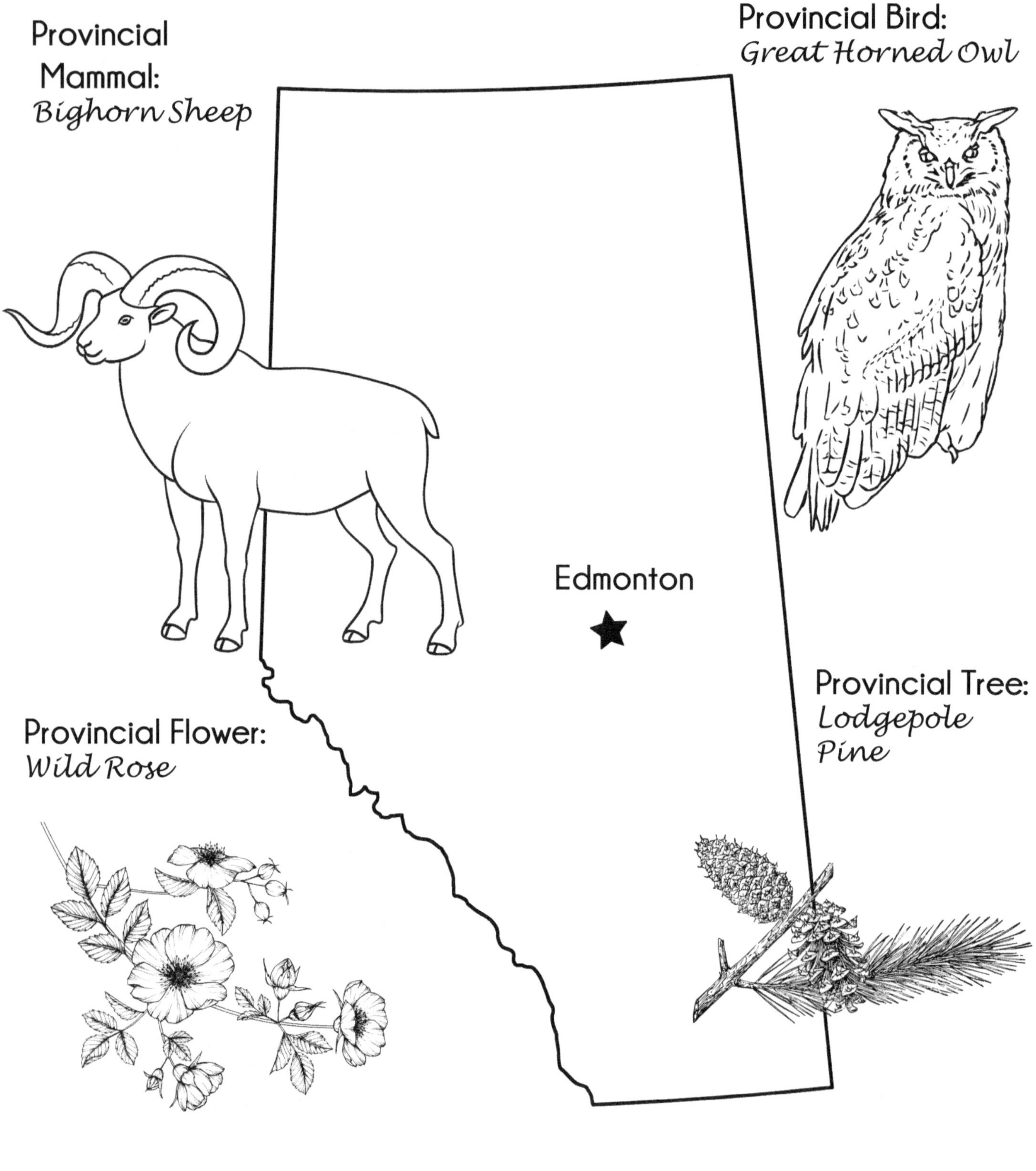

Provincial Mammal: *Bighorn Sheep*

Provincial Bird: *Great Horned Owl*

★ Edmonton

Provincial Flower: *Wild Rose*

Provincial Tree: *Lodgepole Pine*

Facts About Alberta

Capital: Edmonton

Confederation: September 1, 1905

Language(s):   English

Postal Abbreviation: AB

Major Cities: Calgary

Population: 4,262,635

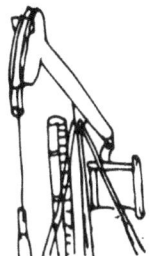

ALBERTA
BANFF
BIGHORN SHEEP
CALGARY
EDMONTON
ELK ISLAND
FOSSILS
LANDLOCKED
OILERS
WILD ROSE

Find the Words

```
B G Q E D M O N T O N U
Z I I I K C K N Z C X I
T V G F A L B E R T A D
E F Y H B R T F T V N O
S O R E O Z U M D A B I
O S A W D R L B L J R L
R S G A W N N S A W G E
D I L N D Y I S Y N Q R
L L A Y G K M S H T F S
I S C M L E J W P E K F
W A C E I V P A H R E P
D E K C O L D N A L I P
```

Things to Know About Alberta

- Sixth largest province by area
- Named after Queen Victoria's daughter
- Has large oil industry
- Grows wheat, barley, canola, oats, other grains
- One of only two landlocked provinces
- Edmonton is home to almost 1 million people
- The West Edmonton Mall is the largest mall in North America and contains the world's largest indoor roller coaster
- Edmonton is nicknamed Festival City
- Calgary is the largest city in Alberta and the fourth largest in Canada with a population of 1.3 million
- Calgary has been named the most livable city in North America
- Calgary is the sunniest city in Canada with an average of 321 days of sun per year
- Alberta has five National Parks: Banff, Elk Island, Jasper, Waterton, and Wood Buffalo

Color the Flag!

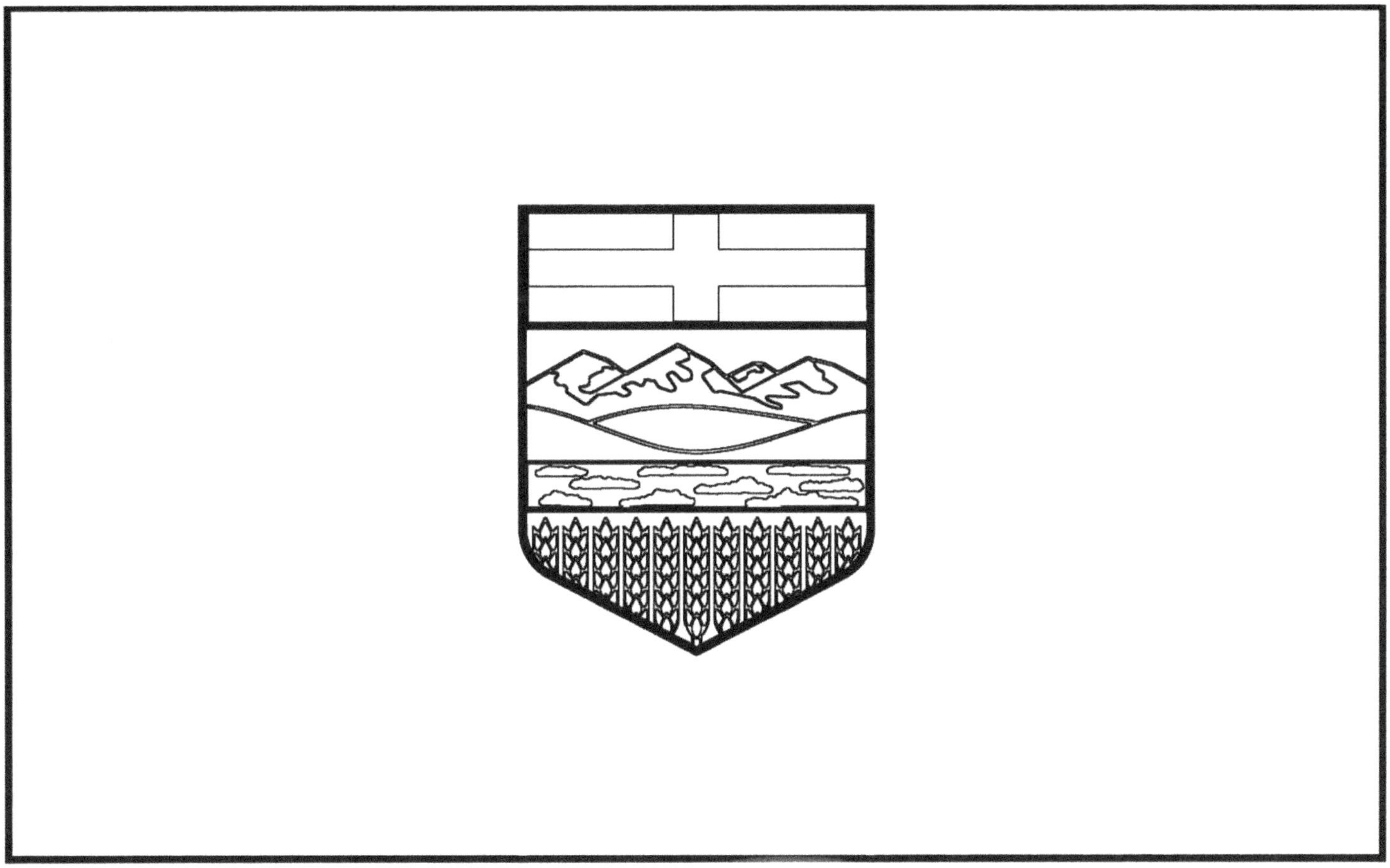

- Mount Columbia is the highest point in Alberta (3,747 meters [12,293 ft] above sea level)
- Home of Dinosaur Provincial Park, one of the best dinosaur fossil spots in North America
- Edmonton Oilers are Alberta's professional hockey team

British Columbia

Motto: *Splendour without Diminishment*

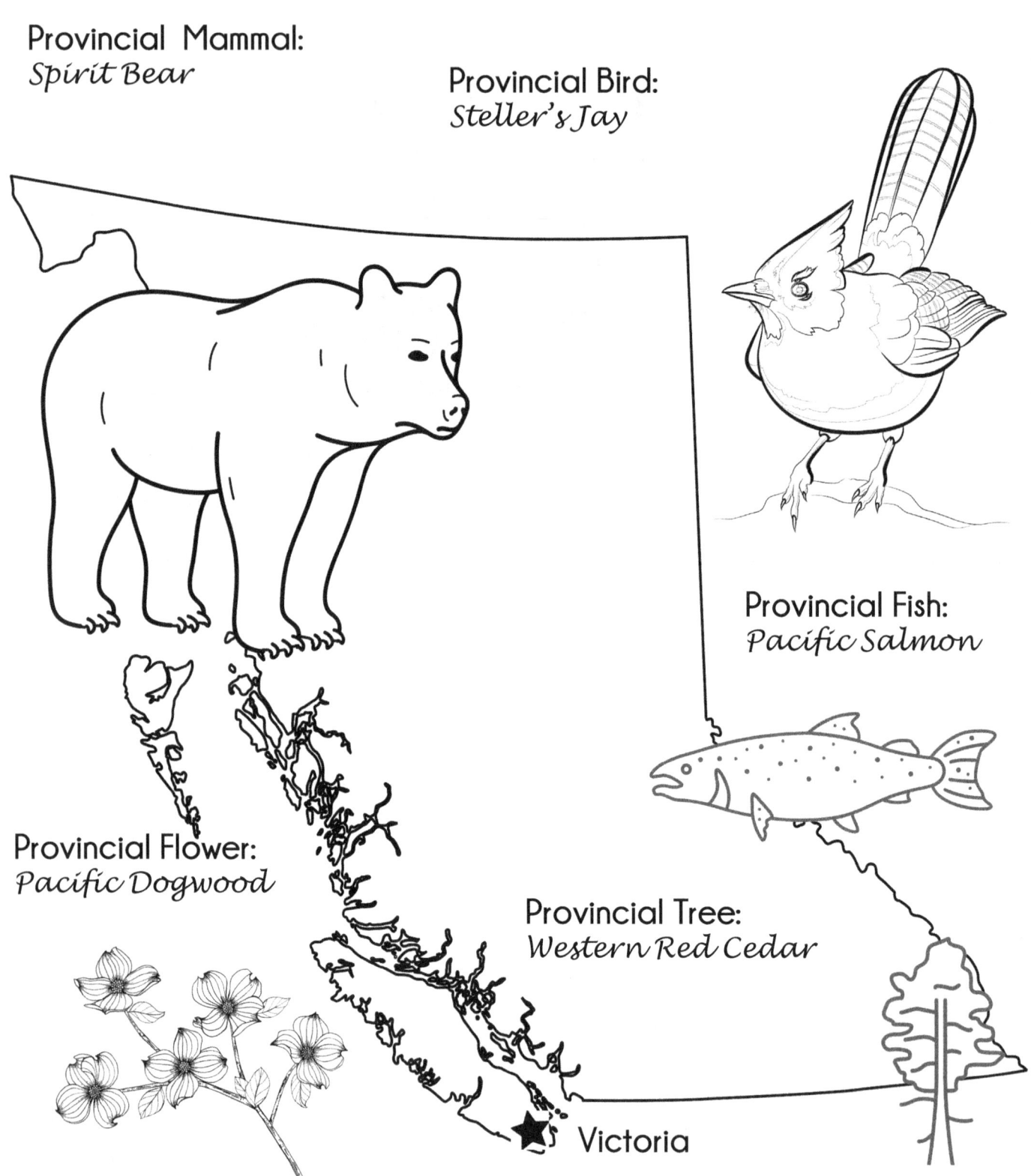

Provincial Mammal: *Spirit Bear*

Provincial Bird: *Steller's Jay*

Provincial Fish: *Pacific Salmon*

Provincial Flower: *Pacific Dogwood*

Provincial Tree: *Western Red Cedar*

Victoria

Facts About British Columbia

Capital: Victoria

Confederation: July 20, 1871

Language(s): English

Postal Abbreviation: BC

Major Cities: Vancouver, Surrey, Burnaby, Richmond, Abbotsford

Population: 5,000,879

DELLA FALLS
DOGWOOD
GULF ISLANDS
LARGEST
PACIFIC
REVELSTOKE
SPIRIT BEAR
VANCOUVER
VICTORIA
WESTERN

Find the Words

```
O N O F J X F F O Q M Y
D D S W B X W W F Q E S
D E L L A F A L L S O P
G U L F I S L A N D S I
W U D O G W O O D J V R
E V A N C O U V E R I I
S L A R G E S T T E C T
T P A C I F I C H C T B
E L K D R M P X Z N O E
R T B E N S L E Q T R A
N W O H W I U X L L I R
R E V E L S T O K E A R
```

Things to Know About British Columbia

- Third largest province by area
- Four times the size of Great Britain
- Western most province
- Over 27,000 kilometers of coastline
- Victoria, the capital, was named after Queen Victoria
- Half of all British Columbians live in the Vancouver area
- Vancouver is the third largest city in Canada
- British Columbia has seven national parks – Glacier, Gulf Islands, Gwaii Haanas, Kootenay, Mount Revelstoke, Pacific Rim, and Yoho
- The Hanging Garden Tree is one of the oldest cedar trees, approximately 1,500 years old
- Mining, forestry, manufacturing, and tourism are the largest industries
- Vancouver is the most expensive city in Canada
- British Columbia was founded during the Gold Rush
- The largest blue whale skeleton is in British Columbia at the Royal British Columbia Museum
- The world's largest totem pole is in Alert Bay, BC

Color the Flag!

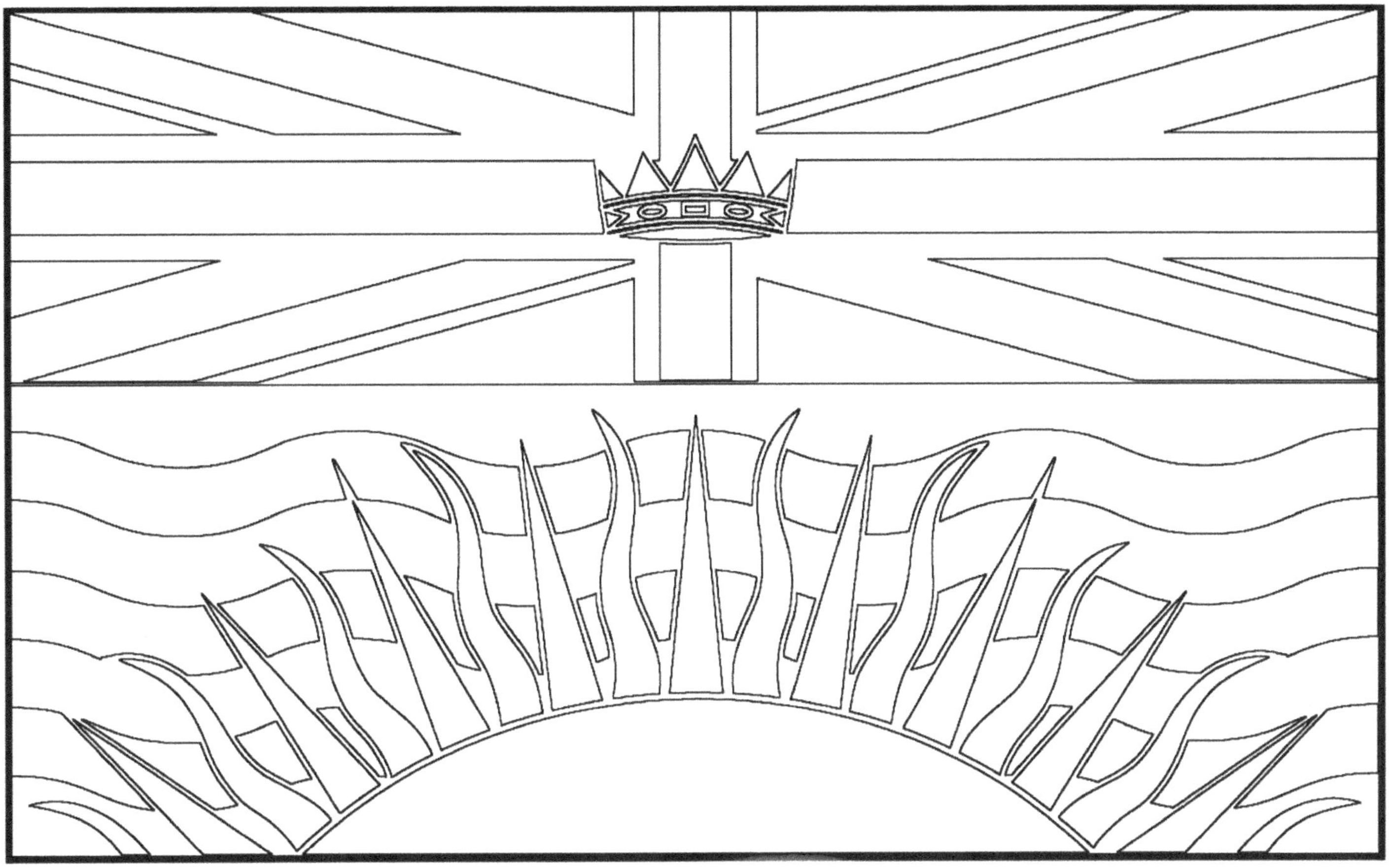

- British Columbia has more than 400 parks and conservation areas 
- Has the mildest climate in Canada
- One of the largest producers of cranberries and blueberries in the world
- Della Falls, on Vancouver Island, is the highest waterfall in Canada

Manitoba

Motto: *Glorious and Free*

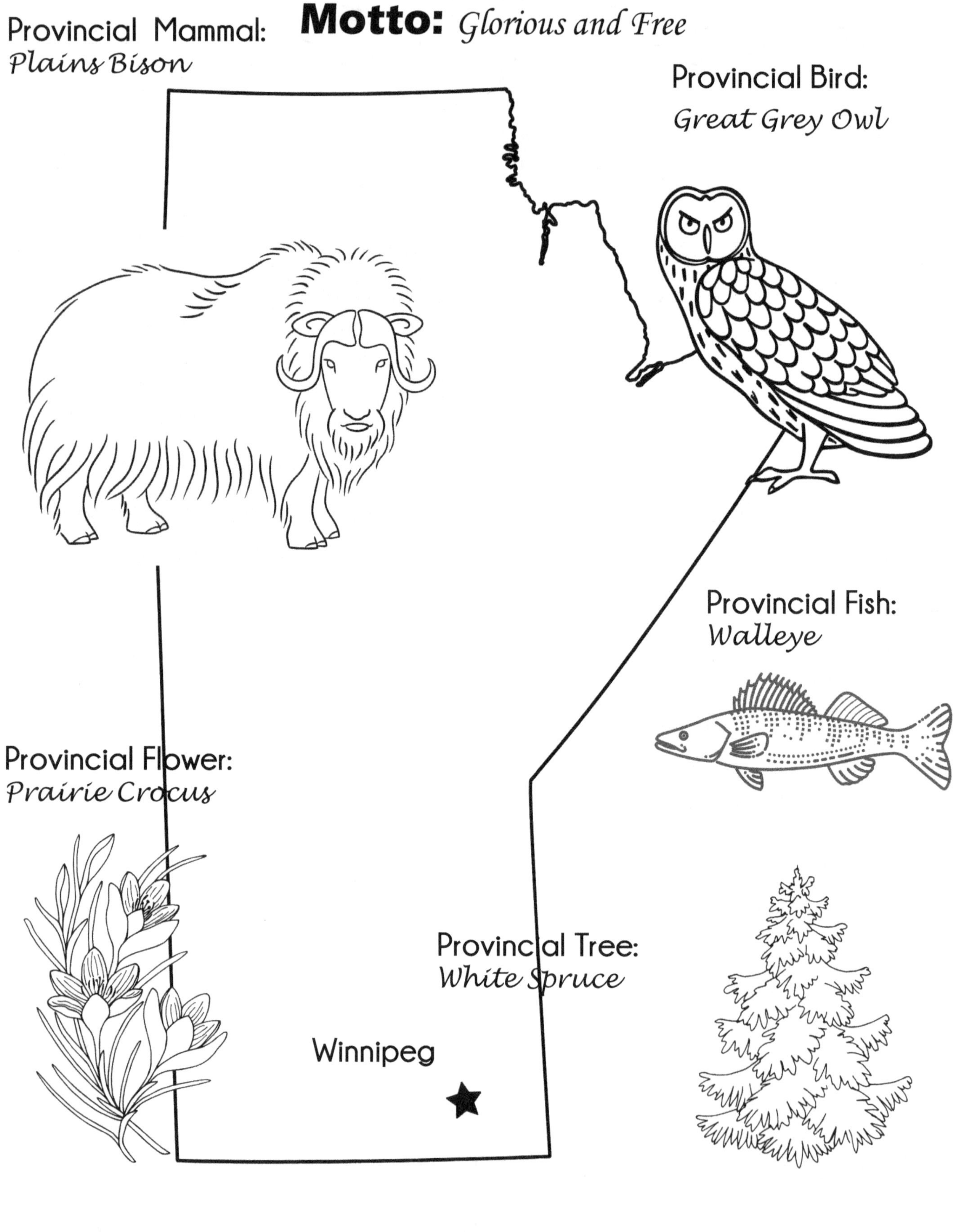

Provincial Mammal:
Plains Bison

Provincial Bird:
Great Grey Owl

Provincial Fish:
Walleye

Provincial Flower:
Prairie Crocus

Provincial Tree:
White Spruce

Winnipeg

Facts About Manitoba

Capital: Winnipeg

Confederation: July 15, 1870

Language(s): English

Postal Abbreviation: MB

Major Cities: Winnipeg, Brandon, Winkler

Population: 1,342,000

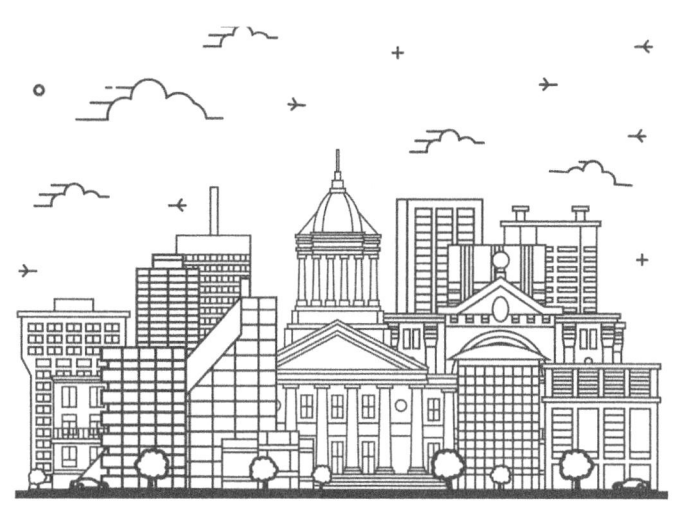

BISON
CHURCHILL
CURLING
HUDSON BAY
LAKES
MANITOBA
POLAR BEAR
PRAIRIE
WINKLER
WINNIPEG

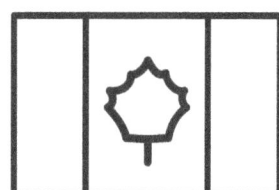

Find the Words

```
W I N N I P E G J B R J
H I G F R F I D A E K L
L A O P S C R L L O L O
A H M F O U U K G I H M
K U A W J L N R H Y N L
E D N H Z I A C L O S J
S S I Y W D R R S I M Q
W O T F Q U X I B Q N O
B N O A H E B D V E S G
K B B C L N F A E J A E
P A A F M D P V C Y B R
B Y P P R A I R I E V B
```

Things to Know About Manitoba

- Manitoba is bordered by Saskatchewan, Ontario, Nunavut, North Dakota, and Minnesota
- One of the three Prairie provinces
- Manitoba is from the Cree language, it means "the narrows of the Great Spirit"
- Home to the Hudson Bay Company, known for fur trade
- Manitoba is large, covering 650,000 square kilometers (251,000 square miles)
- It contains arctic tundra, boreal forests, lakes, and farmland
- Manitoba is a bilingual province
- Winnipeg is the capital and largest city
- Manitoba has a very low population density of just 2.2 people per square kilometer
- Manitoba contains two national parks, Riding Mountain and Wapusk National Parks
- The Northern Lights (aurora borealis) are visible in northern Manitoba from November to April
- The Port of Churchill is the shortest route between North America and Asia
- Lake Winnipeg is the tenth-largest freshwater

Color the Flag!

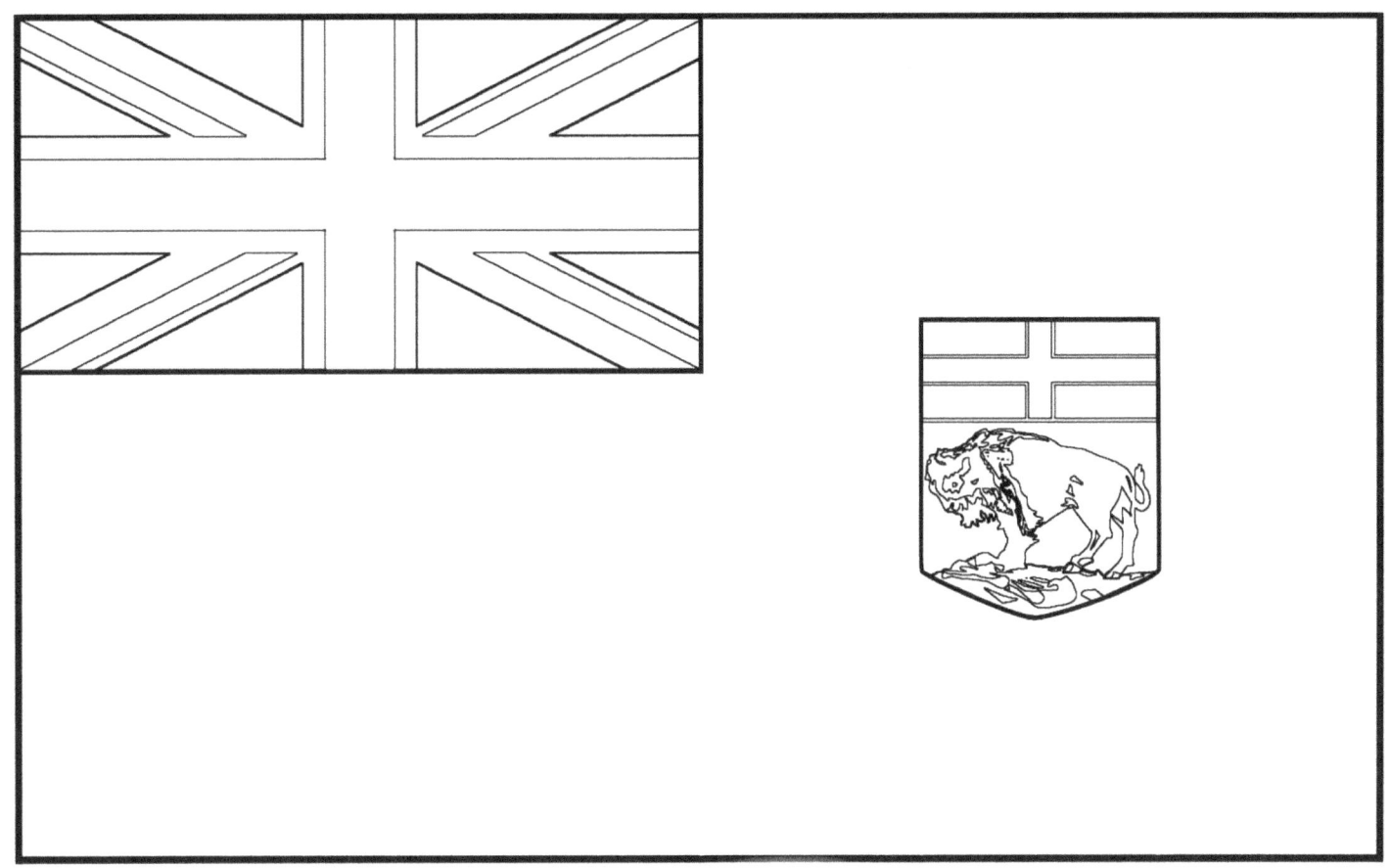

lake in the world

- Hudson Bay is the second-largest bay in the world
- Manitoba contains more than 110,000 lakes
- Winnipeg is one of the sunniest cities in Canada
- Manitoba's Churchill is nicknamed the polar bear capital of the world
- Manitoba is the curling capital of the world
- Manitoba has four professional sports teams: Blue Bombers (football), Jets (hockey), Moose (hockey), and Goldeyes (baseball)

New Brunswick

Motto: *Hope Was Restored*

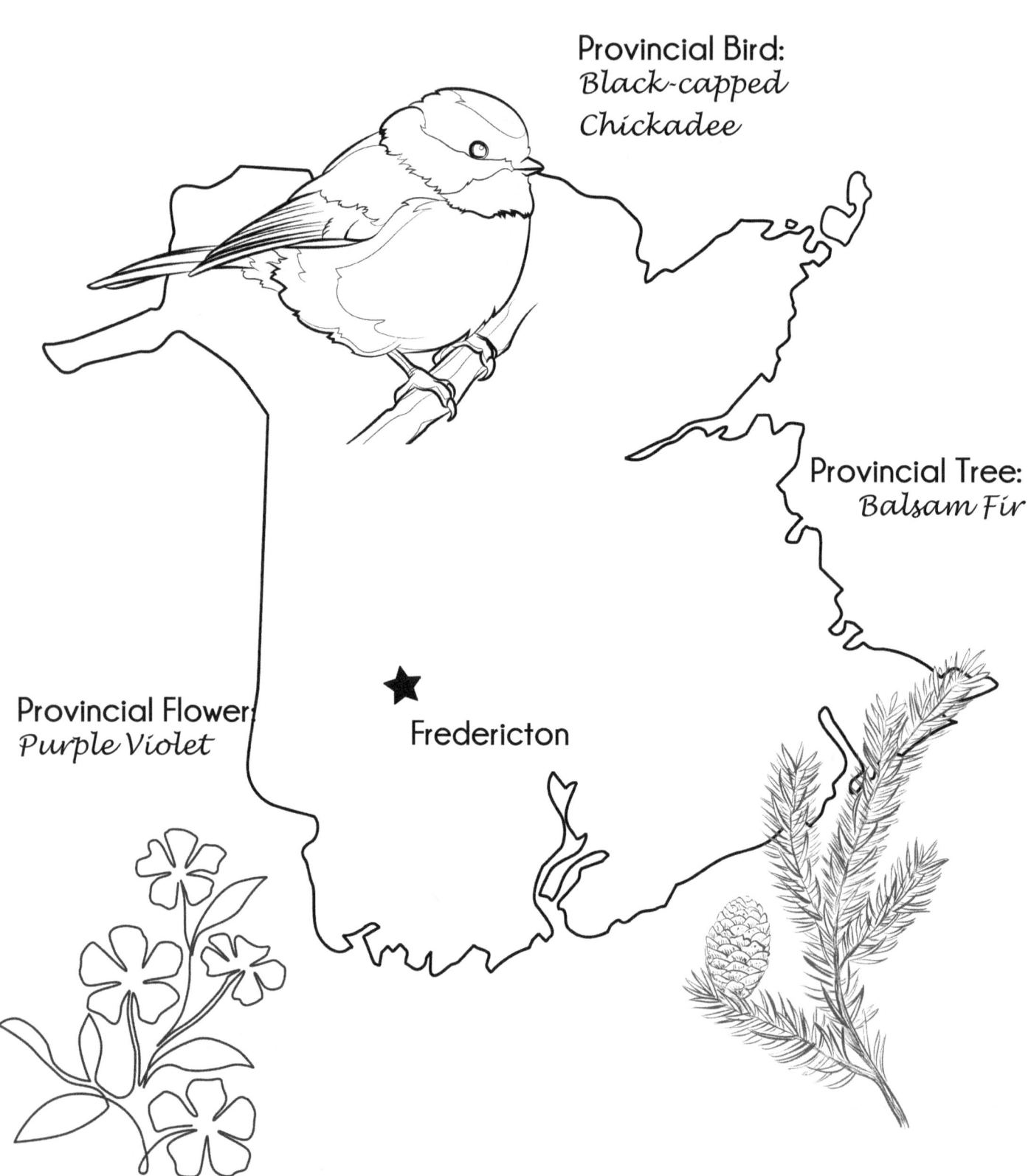

Provincial Bird: *Black-capped Chickadee*

Provincial Tree: *Balsam Fir*

Provincial Flower: *Purple Violet*

Fredericton

Facts About New Brunswick

Capital: Fredericton

Confederation: July 1, 1867

Language(s): English, French

Postal Abbreviation: NB

Major Cities: Moncton, Saint John, Fredericton

Population: 776,000

BALSAM FIR
BAY OF FUNDY
CHICKADEE
FREDERICTON
LIGHTHOUSES
MARITIME
MONCTON
OLD SOW
SAINT JOHN
WHALES

Find the Words

```
K E S U N L O L D S O W
B Y S K B I W H A L E S
A K A R J G G B Y C G D
Y M I M E H G A D H K R
O A N O D T W L O I B P
F R T N A H M S R C G U
F I J C K O R A A K G A
U T O T U U Y M A A J F
N I H O D S O F D D R C
D M N N U E H I Y E D U
Y E Z Z O S C R P E G Q
F R E D E R I C T O N J
```

Things to Know About New Brunswick

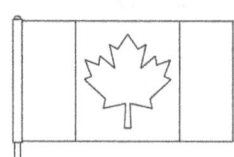

- Largest of the three Maritime Provinces
- Only officially bilingual province
- The Bay of Fundy has the highest tides on the planet
- Grand Manan Island is one of the top birding areas of North America
- New Brunswick has more than 60 lighthouses
- The Bay of Fundy is home to many species of whales including humpbacks, pilot, and finback whales

- New Brunswick is the covered bridge capital of Canada
- The warmest saltwater beaches in Canada are located here
- The snow blower was invented in New Brunswick in 1870
- Home to the world's largest lobster, a sculpture that is 11 meters (35 feet) long, located in Shediac, the Lobster Capital of the World
- The second largest whirlpool in the world,

Color the Flag!

called "Old Sow" is located between Deer and Indian Islands

- The University of New Brunswick was established in 1785 and is tied with the University of Georgia for the oldest university in North America
- The Saint John River flows backwards twice per day, every day
- Saint John is Canada's oldest incorporated city
- The first female ship captain in North America, Molly Kool, was from Alma, New Brunswick

Newfoundland and Labrador

Motto: *Seek ye first the Kingdom of God*

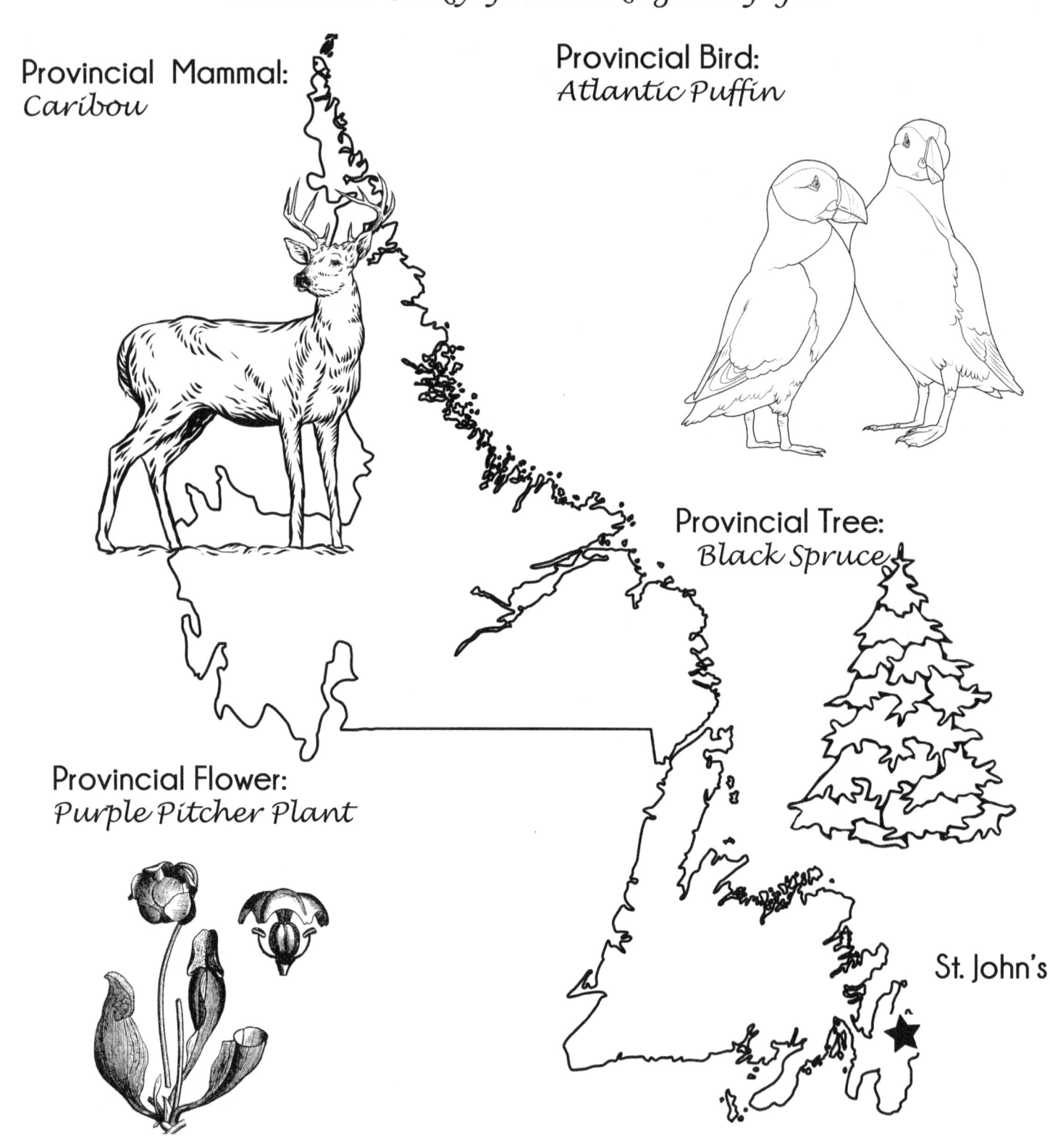

Provincial Mammal: Caribou

Provincial Bird: Atlantic Puffin

Provincial Tree: Black Spruce

Provincial Flower: Purple Pitcher Plant

St. John's

Facts About Newfoundland and Labrador

Capital: St. John's

Confederation: March 31, 1949

Language(s): English

Postal Abbreviation: NL

Major Cities: St. John's, Corner Brook, Mount Pearl

Population: 510,555

CARIBOU
CAUBVICK
EASTERN
ISLANDS
LABRADOR
NEWFOUNDLAND
PUFFIN
ST. JOHN'S
TITANIC
VIKINGS

Find the Words

```
N A L R V S U C L J J C
F E P U F F I N A Z S A
I B W D O I S K B I T R
X S G F A N C O R N J I
C C L Y O I C N A H O B
F S S A V U R X D A H O
U O Y B N E N W O P N U
J T U L T D P D R S S E
Y A Y S J G S L L L A K
C J A U Z I Q L D A M B
N E C V I K I N G S N U
J R T I T A N I C G T D
```

Things to Know About Newfoundland and Labrador

- The first province to respond to the Titanic distress signal
- The most easterly province in Canada
- The province contains more than 7,000 small islands
- More than 90 percent of the population lives on the island of Newfoundland
- St. John's is North America's easternmost city
- The landscape was shaped during the ice ages when glaciers created a ragged coastline and, deep fjords, and rocky cliffs
- Mount Caubvick is the highest point in the province at 1,652 meters (5,420 feet)

- The province contains four national parks – Gros Morne, Terra Nova, Torngat Mountains, and Dungeon Provincial Park
- Humans have inhabited Newfoundland and Labrador for at least 9,000 years
- The Vikings first settled in L'Anse aux Meadows in 1000 AD

Color the Flag!

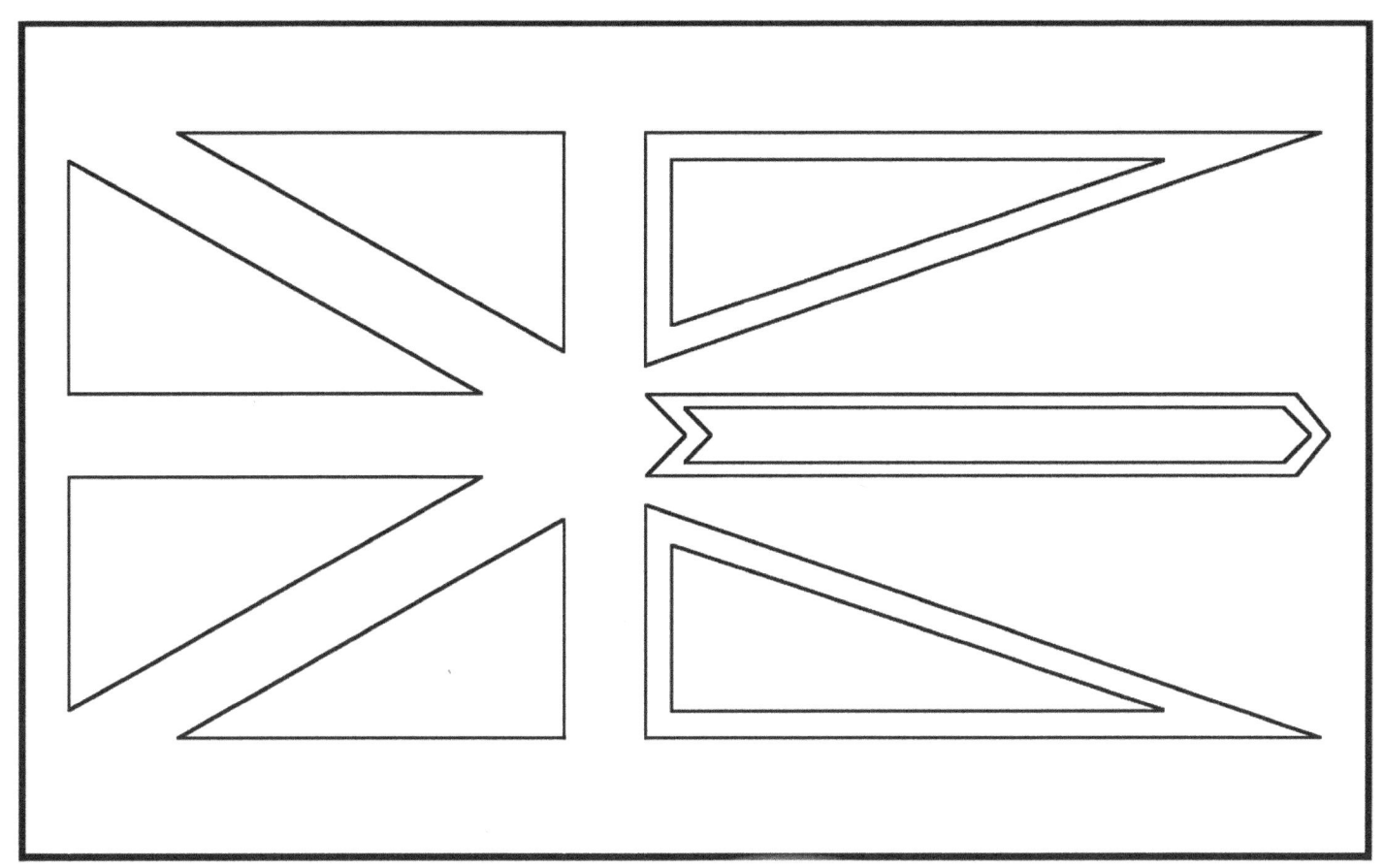

- St. John's is the oldest settlement in Canada, dating to 1497
- The Royal St. John's Regatta is one of the oldest sporting events in Canada
- The first nonstop transatlantic flight took off from St. John's and landed in Clifden, Ireland

Northwest Territories

Motto: *None*

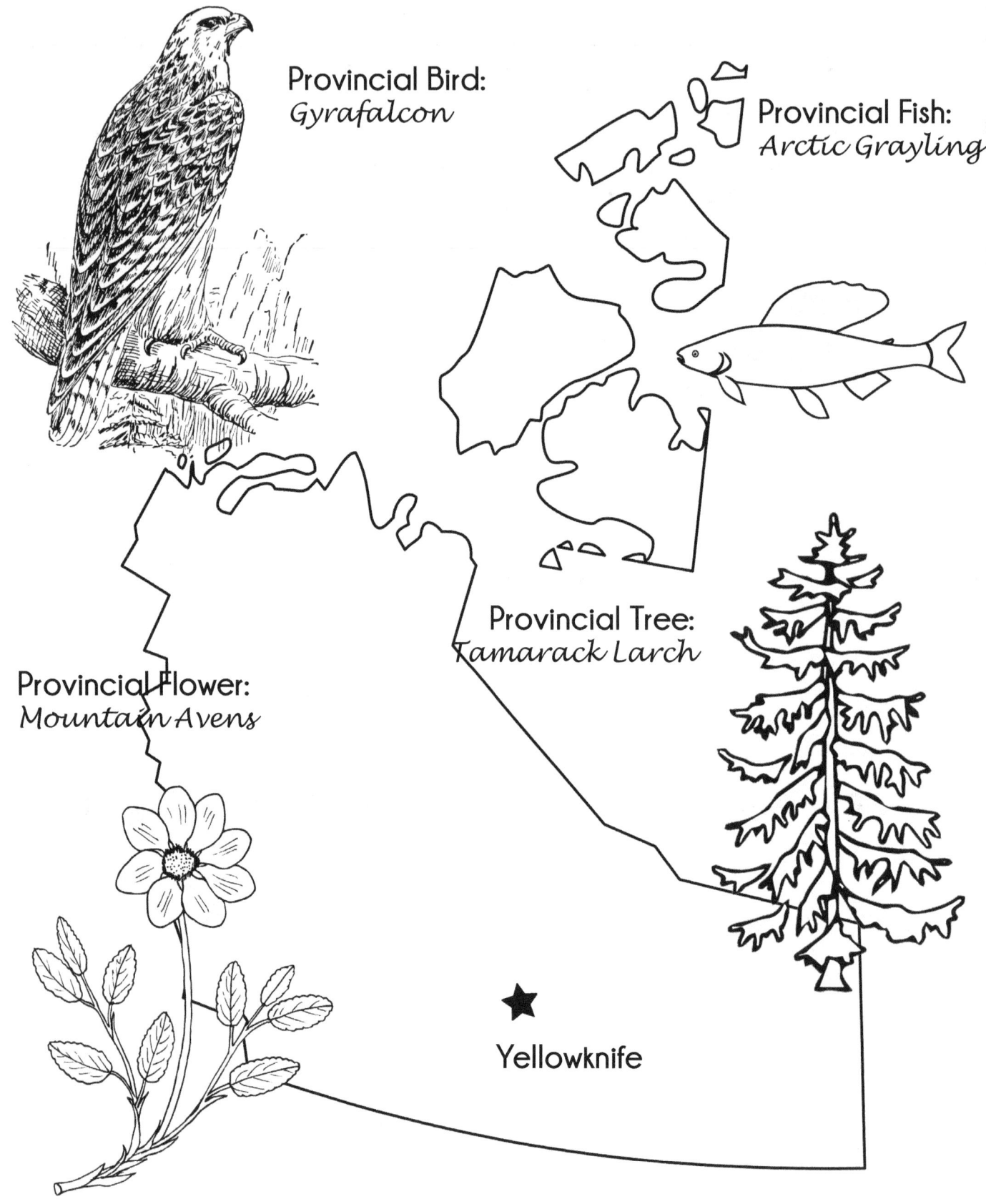

Provincial Bird: *Gyrafalcon*

Provincial Fish: *Arctic Grayling*

Provincial Tree: *Tamarack Larch*

Provincial Flower: *Mountain Avens*

★ Yellowknife

Facts About Northwest Territories

Capital: Yellowknife

Confederation: July 15, 1870

Language(s): Chipewyan, Cree, English, French, Gwich'in, Inuinnaqtun, Inuktitut, Inuvialuktun, North Slavey, South Slavey, Tlicho

Postal Abbreviation: NT

Major Cities: Yellowknife

Population: 41,070

ARCTIC CIRCLE
GRAYLING
NAHANNI
NORTH POLE
NORTHERN LIGHTS
NORTHWEST
POLAR NIGHT
SUNLIGHT
VIRGINIA FALLS
YELLOWKNIFE

Find the Words

```
A R C T I C C I R C L E O D
O I B C G R A Y L I N G U X
X P M P O L A R N I G H T B
N O R T H E R N L I G H T S
S U N L I G H T B I R W L P
L P X Y E L L O W K N I F E
X C H H N O R T H P O L E B
G Y I M S O X D J G N S J R
G U N O R T H W E S T M R C
T N A H A N N I L R E P X U
H V I R G I N I A F A L L S
```

Things to Know About Northwest Territories

- The territory extends way above the Arctic Circle
- It has the second lowest population density of any province or territory in Canada at only .4 people per square kilometer
- This area is one of the best in the world for viewing the Northern Lights
- The land of the Midnight Sun, Yellowknife gets more than 20 hours of sunlight in June and never gets fully dark
- Conversely, in the winter is remains dark virtually all the time, known as polar night
- Temperatures can be extreme, with summers getting hot (25 to 32 degrees Celsius) and winters getting very cold (-40 to -20 degrees Celsius)
- Yellowknife is one of the closest cities in the world to the North Pole
- Great Slave Lake is the second largest lake within Canada and the ninth largest lake in the world; it is roughly the size of the country of Belgium and is the deepest lake in North America at 614 meters (2,014 feet)

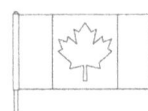

Color the Flag!

- Nahanni National Park was established in 1976 and is one of the first UNESCO world heritage sites
- Great Bear Lake is the largest lake located entirely within Canada
- Virginia Falls, located in Nahanni National Park, are almost twice the height of Niagara Falls
- Inuvik, meaning "place of people," is the largest town in Northwest Territory north of the Arctic Circle
- There are 11 official languages in the Northwest Territory

Nova Scotia

Motto: One Defends and the Other Conquers

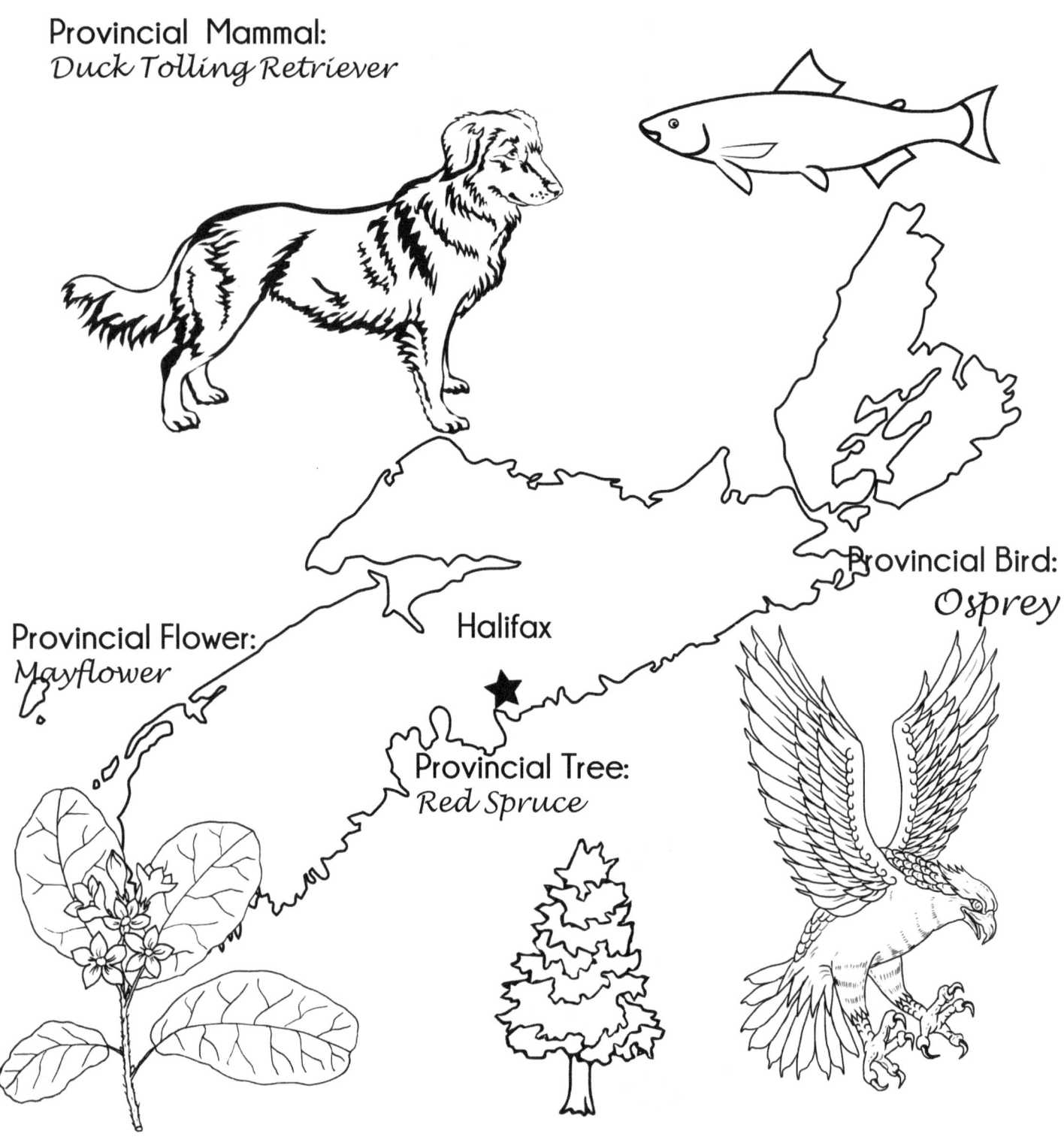

Provincial Fish: Brook Trout

Provincial Mammal: Duck Tolling Retriever

Provincial Bird: Osprey

Provincial Flower: Mayflower

Halifax

Provincial Tree: Red Spruce

Facts About Nova Scotia

Capital: Halifax

Confederation: July 1, 1867

Language(s): English

Postal Abbreviation: NS

Major Cities: Halifax, Cape Breton-Sydney, Truro, New Glasgow

Population: 970,000

ACADIA
BLUENOSERS
BROOK TROUT
GLACE BAY
HALIFAX
LOBSTER
NOVA SCOTIA
OSPREY
PORT ROYAL
WHITE HILL

Find the Words

```
B B L U E N O S E R S V
R W N L T R F Z R P X U
O H T C T B C M C D D U
O I N O V A S C O T I A
K T G L W H O P E O U Y
T E L A O D A S N A L G
R H A C C B K L P I N O
O I C A A Q S H I R E R
U L E D M W W T N F E G
T L B I E U P H E Q A Y
Q I A A B I N T R R Z X
T O Y P O R T R O Y A L
```

Things to Know About Nova Scotia

- The name Nova Scotia is Latin for New Scotland
- It is the second smallest province in land area with 53,000 square km (20,500 square miles)
- It contains 13,300 km of coastline and is nicknamed the Ocean Playground
- The flag of Novia Scotia is a reversal of the flag of Scotland
- Nova Scotians are nicknamed Bluenosers
- Indigenous Mi'kmaq people lived in the area for at least 5,000 years before Europeans first landed in Nova Scotia in 1497
- French colonists were the first to establish a settlement in 1605 in Port Royal, now known as Acadia
- Nova Scotia is one of the founding four provinces of Canada
- Nova Scotia is one of the best places in the world to go whale watching with over 12 species of whale
- Lobster from Nova Scotia waters is world famous
- The hills and small mountains in the province are part of the Appalachian Mountains, which extend all the way into the southern United States
- White Hill is the highest point in the province at 532 meters (1,745 feet) above sea level
- Nova Scotia has some of the mildest weather

Color the Flag!

in Canada but can still get extremely cold in winter and very hot in the summer

- The first wireless message from North America to Europe was sent from Glace Bay, Cape Breton by Guglielmo Marconi in 1902
- The Christmas Tree capital of Canada is Chester, Nova Scotia
- There are more than 150 lighthouses in the province

Nunavut

Motto: *Nunavut, Our Strength*

Provincial Mammal: *Canadian Inuit Dog*

Provincial Bird: *Rock Ptarmigan*

Provincial Flower: *Purple Saxifrage*

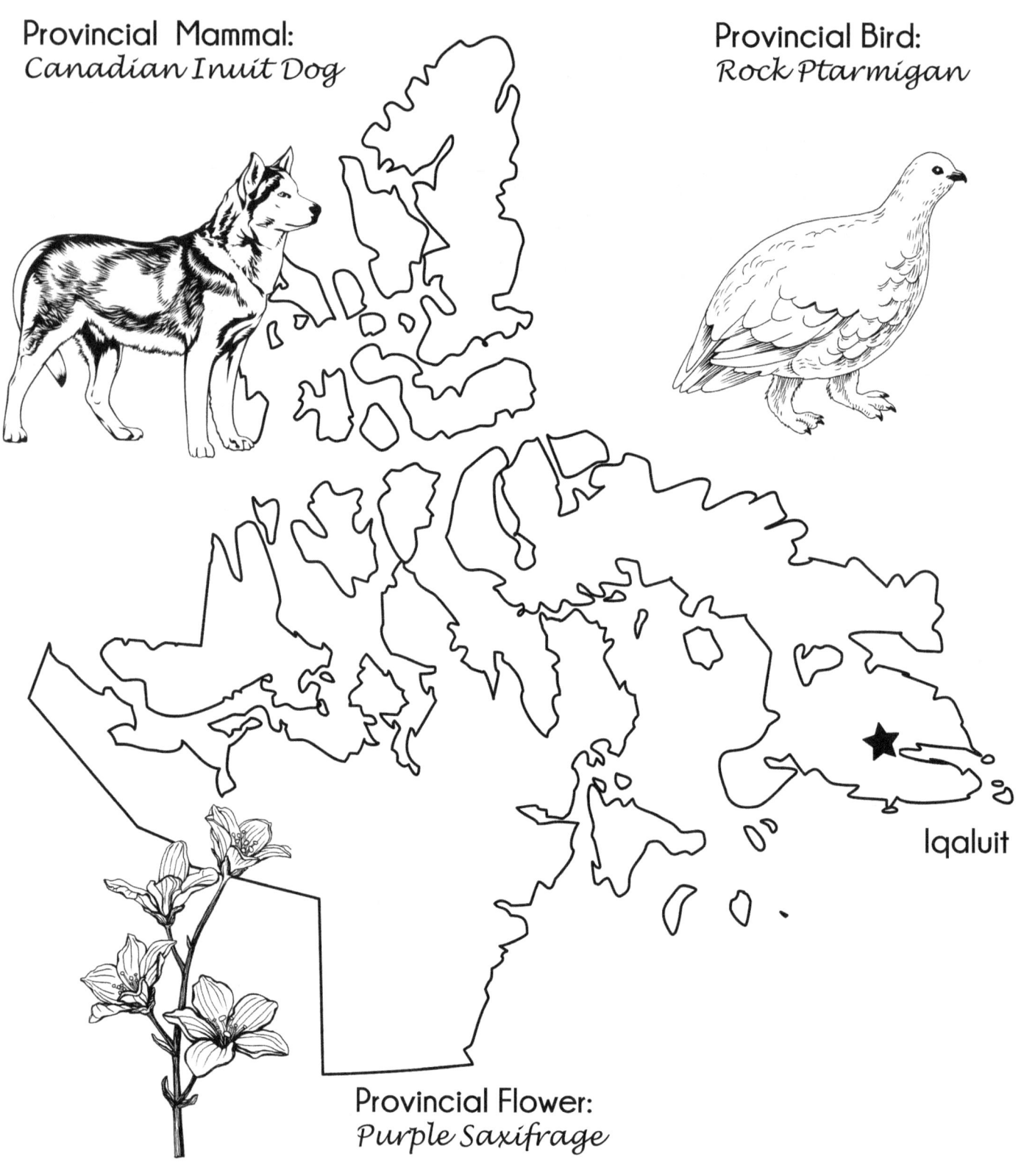

Iqaluit

Facts About Nunavut

Capital: Iqaluit

Confederation: April 1, 1999

Language(s): Inuinnaqtun, Inuktitut, English, French

Postal Abbreviation: NU

Major Cities: Iqaluit

Population: 36,858

ALERT
BAFFIN ISLAND
BARBEAU PEAK
COASTLINE
INUIT DOG
IQALUIT
NARWHALS
NORTH
NUNAVUT
TUNDRA

Find the Words

```
I C C O A S T L I N E D
Q B I N U I T D O G N A
A S A Z R J D K M A N L
L W Q R H E R M L P A E
U L X Z B N A S Z T R R
I G S F I E I L U W W T
T N J E T N A V Z D H A
G B H F I U A U G R A Q
X V I F G N N S P C L D
T D F D U B Y D A E S G
C A V N V I K Q R K A M
B J L Z N O R T H A K K
```

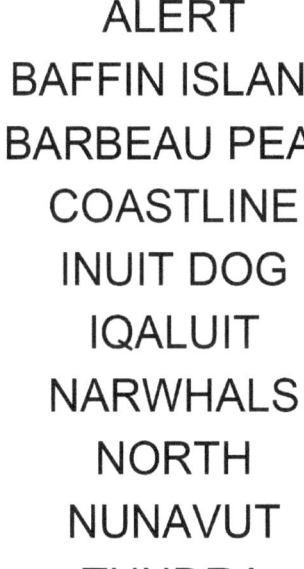

Things to Know About Nunavut

- Largest territory with an area of 2,093,190 square kilometers (about 1 million square miles)
- About 75 percent of the world's narwhal population migrate into Nunavut's bays and estuaries
- The name of the capital, Iqaluit, means "place of fish"
- Taxis in Iqaluit charge a flat rate of $8 to go anywhere
- Barbeau Peak on Ellesmere Island is the highest point in Nunavut at 2,616 meters (8,583 feet) above sea level
- Alert, Nunavut is the world's most northern permanently inhabited place
- Nunavut has five national parks – Auyuittuq, Qausuittuq, Quttinirpaaq, Tuktut Nogait, and Ukkusiksalik national parks
- Nunavut has under 32 kilometers of paved roads. Planes, boats, and snowmobiles are popular ways of getting around
- Baffin Island is the fifth largest island in the world

Color the Flag!

- Nunavut has the longest coastline in Canada
- There are over 36,000 islands in Nunavut
- There are hardly any trees in Nunavut (only in the southernmost parts) and none on the tundra

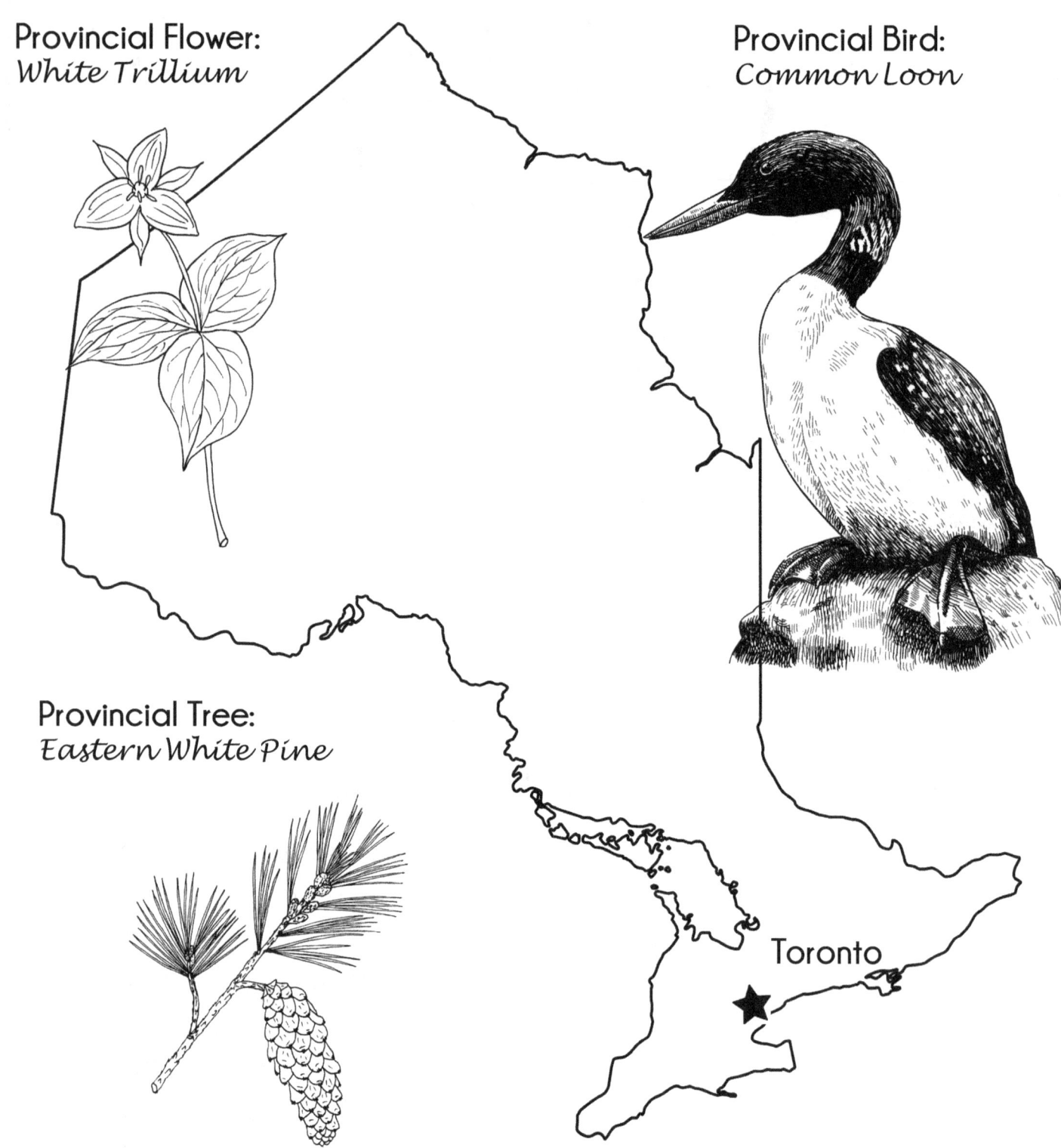

Facts About Ontario

Capital: Toronto

Confederation: July 1, 1867

Language(s): English

Postal Abbreviation: ON

Major Cities: Toronto, Ottawa, Hamilton, Kitchener

Population: 14,224,000

AGRICULTURE
FRESHWATER
NIAGARA FALLS
OKTOBERFEST
ONTARIO
OTTAWA
PELEE ISLANDS
RIDEAU CANAL
TORONTO
WATERFALLS

Find the Words

```
C G J K B O T T A W A R
S L L A F R E T A W T G
P E L E E I S L A N D S
V A G R I C U L T U R E
A J R E T A W H S E R F
X X D B K B Z C A A M I
S L L A F A R A G A I N
O R I D E A U C A N A L
H N A H S A N D J I Z X
T V B D O I R A T N O E
U T S E F R E B O T K O
X Y T T O R O N T O S L
```

Things to Know About Ontario

- Ontario is the second-largest province, with an area of more than one million square kilometers (415,000 square miles) making it larger than Spain and France combined
- Ontario has more than 250,000 lakes and approximately 20 percent of earth's freshwater stores
- Agriculture is big in Ontario with more than 50,000 farms

- Corn, apples, potatoes, soybeans, grains, and more are grown here
- The name Ontario means "beautiful water" in Iroquois
- Niagara Falls is one of North America's most popular tourist destinations; it is made up of three waterfalls which together form the second largest waterfall in the world
- Almost 40 percent of Canadians live in Ontario
- Ishpatina Ridge is the highest point in Ontario at 693 meters (2,250 feet) above sea level
- Canada's most southerly point, Pelee Island is in Ontario
- Ontario can have extreme weather with summer

Color the Flag!

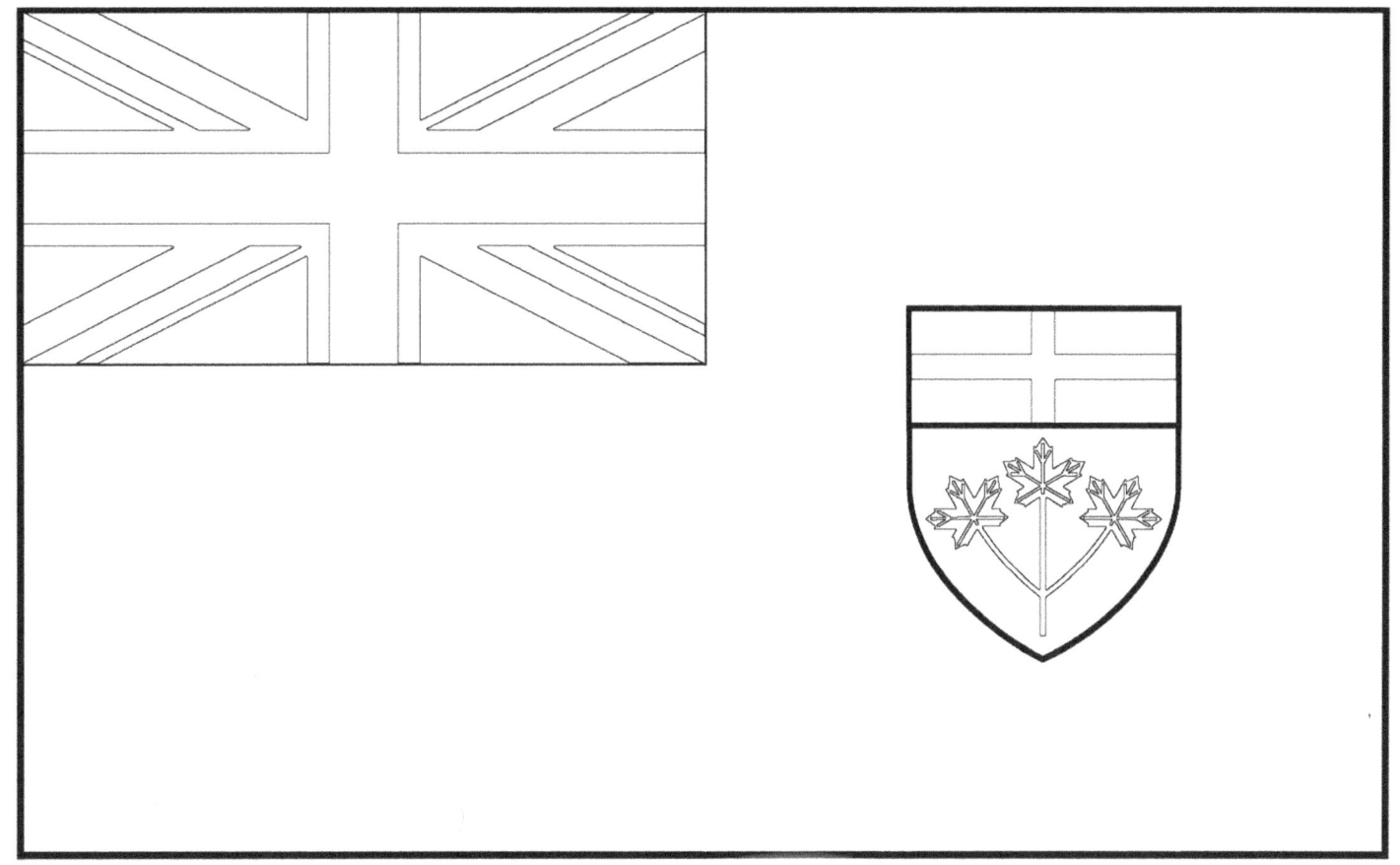

highs above 30 degrees Celsius (86F) and winter lows below -40 degrees Celsius (-40F)

- Kitchener, Ontario is home to the largest Oktoberfest outside of Germany
- The city of Hamilton is nicknamed the Waterfall Capital of the World with more than 100 waterfalls
- Toronto is one of the most multicultural cities in the world with over 140 languages and dialects spoken
- Ottawa's Rideau Canal freezes in winter to become the world's longest skating rink (7.8 km)

Prince Edward Island

Motto: *The Small Under the Protection of the Great*

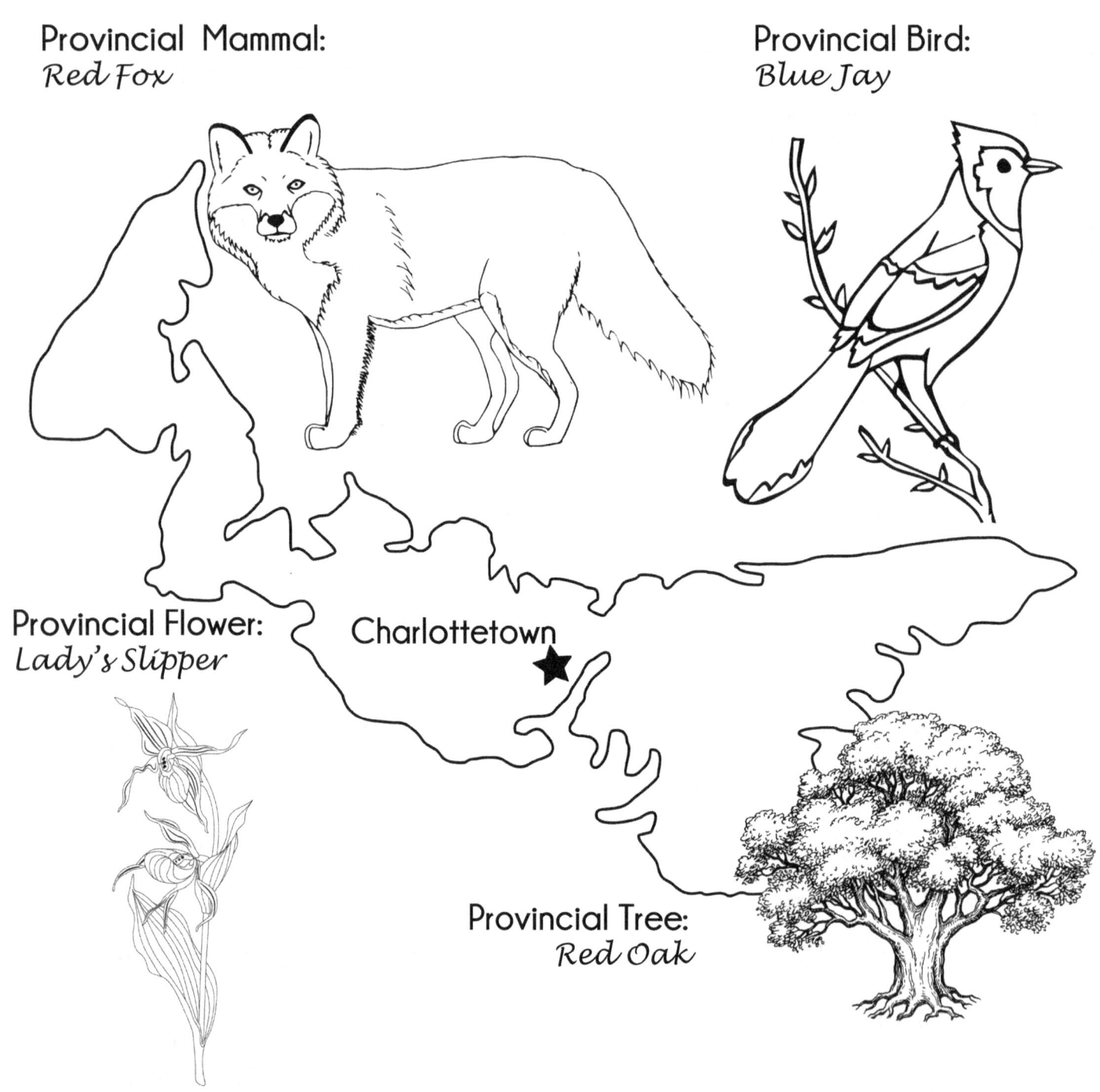

Provincial Mammal: *Red Fox*

Provincial Bird: *Blue Jay*

Provincial Flower: *Lady's Slipper*

Charlottetown

Provincial Tree: *Red Oak*

Facts About Prince Edward Island

Capital: Charlottetown

Confederation: July 1, 1873

Language(s): English

Postal Abbreviation: PE

Major Cities: Charlottetown, Summerside

Population: 154,331

BEACHES
BLUE JAY
CARTIER
CAVENDISH
ISLANDERS
LADY SLIPPER
POTATOES
SAND DUNES
SUMMERSIDE
TOURISM

Find the Words

```
C A V E N D I S H O U Z
L I S L A N D E R S H E
Q A T T T W N A R H D G
P S D V O H D E Q I P P
R A R Y Y U I G S W Y O
W N F J S T R R P A U T
P D D E R L E I J Z J A
G D L A F M I E S X Q T
I U C V M B U P O M H O
E N S U O L W I P H Z E
C E S B B R L D I E J S
N S L B E A C H E S R C
```

Things to Know About Prince Edward Island

- Prince Edward Island (PEI) is Canada's smallest province by land area and population
- The people who live there are referred to as "Islanders"
- It is one of the three Maritime Provinces
- The island was discovered by Europeans in 1534 by Jacques Cartier
- The Mk'kmaq people have lived on the islands for more than 12,000 years
- Charlottetown was once a popular summertime retreat for British nobility
- PEI has more than 1100 kilometers of shoreline including over 800 kilometers of beach
- The Confederation Bridge links the island to New Brunswick and takes 10 minutes to cross; it is the longest bridge over frozen water in the world
- Agriculture, tourism, and fishing are the main industries
- It is the largest potato producing region in Canada, growing more than 20 percent of all potatoes in the country
- Almost all (99 percent) of power generation on the island is from wind farms which supply 15 percent of the electricity used on the island

Color the Flag!

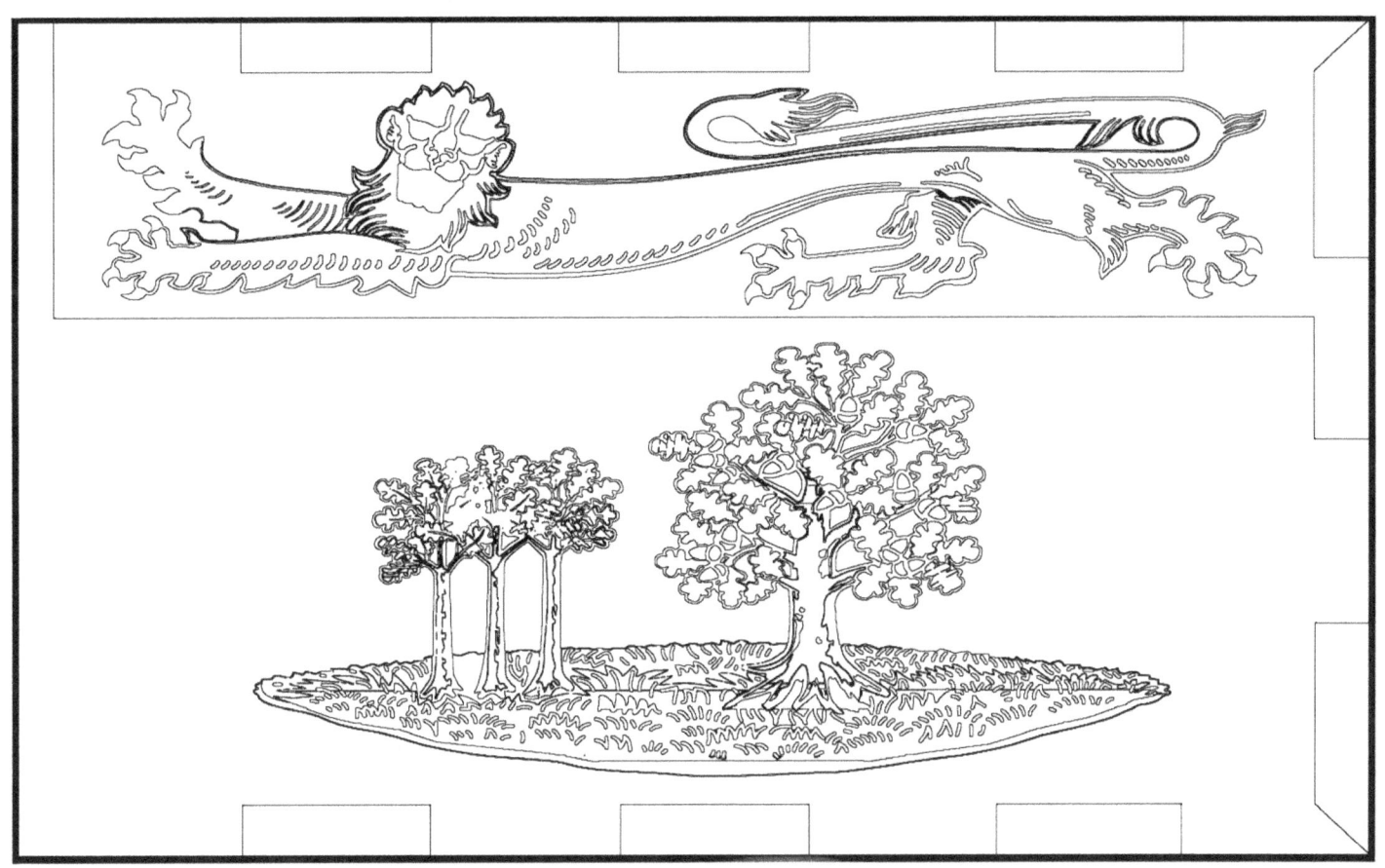

- The popular novel, *Anne of Green Gables*, was set on the island in Cavendish
- Temperatures in winter can reach -35 degrees Celsius (-31F)
- Prince Edward Island consists of 231 minor islands in addition to the main island
- The main industries on the island are agriculture, tourism, and fisheries
- Prince Edward Island National Park is the only national park in the province, it is known for its large sand dunes
- Curling is a popular sport on PEI
- There are over 33 golf courses on the island

Quebec

Motto: *Je me souviens (I Remember)*

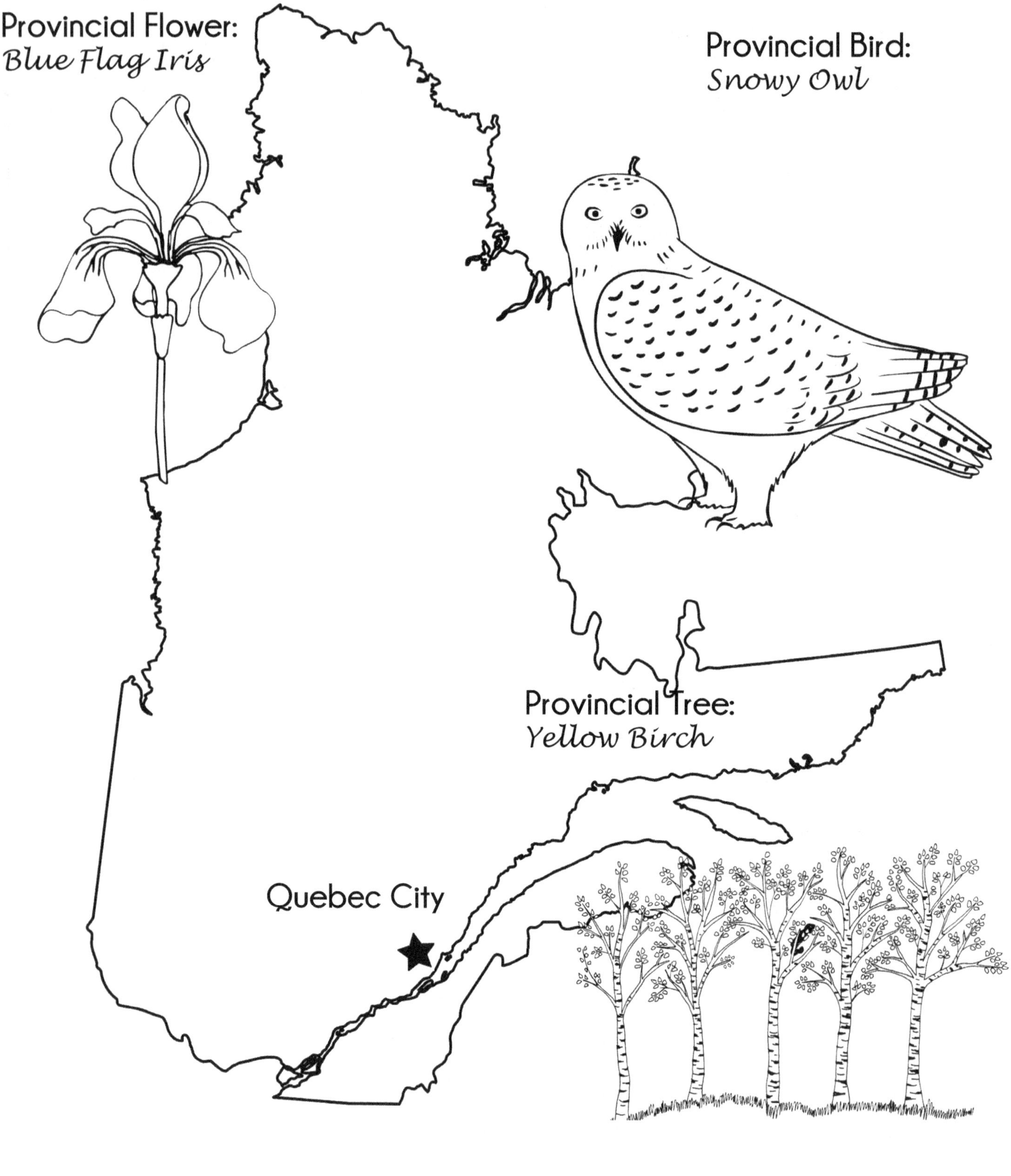

Provincial Flower: *Blue Flag Iris*

Provincial Bird: *Snowy Owl*

Provincial Tree: *Yellow Birch*

Quebec City

Facts About Quebec

Capital: Quebec City

Confederation: July 1, 1867

Language(s): French

Postal Abbreviation: QC

Major Cities: Montreal, Quebec City, Gatineau, Sherbrooke

Population: 8,500,000

CARNIVAL
CHAMPLAIN
CULTURE
FLEUR DE LIS
FRENCH
FRONTENAC
HISTORIC
MAPLE SYRUP
MONTREAL
QUEBEC

Find the Words

```
F Y T Z H J E S V A M J
L L E C H A M P L A I N
E L X F N Y U S J T G U
U F K K F R E N C H R T
R R M A P L E S Y R U P
D O Q F K S S N Y T P C
E N F C A R N I V A L U
L T M O N T R E A L S L
I E L B T B E D L P E T
S N U G Q Q U E B E C U
O A O L Z N I L G H O R
O C S H I S T O R I C E
```

Things to Know About Quebec

- Quebec is the largest Canadian province in area and second-largest in population
- The explorer Jacques Cartier claimed Quebec for France in 1534
- The fleur-de-lis is a popular Quebec symbol; it is also a symbol of the French monarchy
- It is the only province with a majority of French speakers
- Quebec borders the provinces of Ontario, Newfoundland and Labrador, and New Brunswick, as well as four US states – Maine, New Hampshire, New York, and Vermont
- Samuel de Champlain founded Quebec City in 1608
- Quebec City is the only walled city in North America
- Fairmont Le Château Frontenac is the most photographed hotel in the world
- Notre-Dame de Québec is the oldest church in Canada
- The Winter Carnival in Quebec City takes place every February and is the oldest winter festival of its kind
- Montreal is known as the cultural capital of Canada

Color the Flag!

- Montreal was once known as the Paris of North America because of its cobblestone streets, historic architecture, and many cafes
- Quebec produces nearly three-quarters of the world's maple syrup
- Montmorency Falls, near Quebec City, is 30 meters higher than Niagara Falls
- Quebec contains three national parks – Forillon, La Mauricie, and Mingan Archipelago National Park

Saskatchewan

Motto: *From Many Peoples Strength*

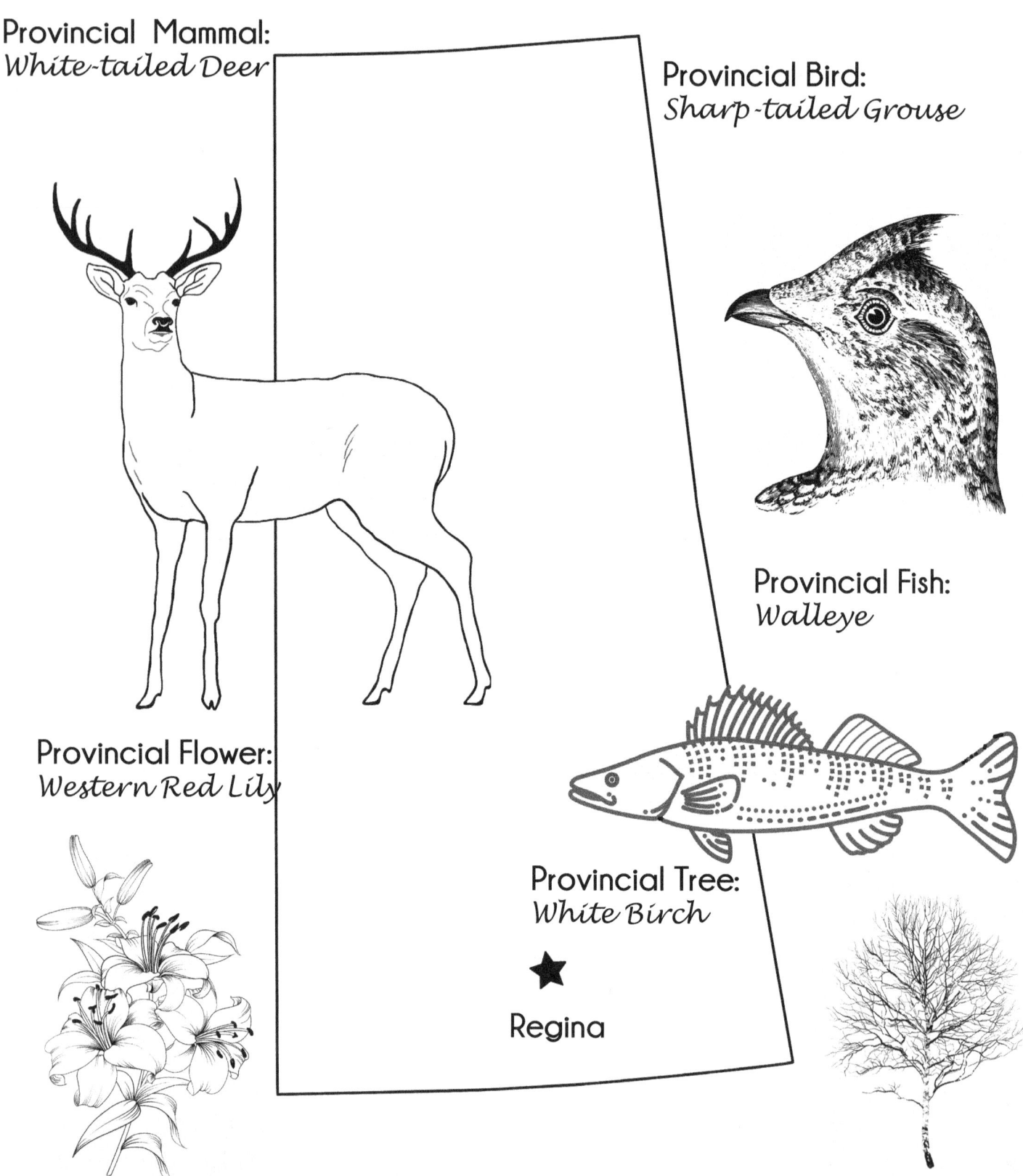

Provincial Mammal: *White-tailed Deer*

Provincial Bird: *Sharp-tailed Grouse*

Provincial Fish: *Walleye*

Provincial Flower: *Western Red Lily*

Provincial Tree: *White Birch*

★ Regina

Facts About Saskatchewan

Capital: Regina

Confederation: September 1, 1905

Language(s): English

Postal Abbreviation: SK

Major Cities: Saskatoon, Regina, Prince Albert, Moose Jaw

Population: 1,132,505

ATHABASCA
FOSSILS
LIVING SKIES
MANITOU
POTASH
PRINCE ALBERT
PURPLE BEACH
REGINA
SASKATOON
WHEAT

Find the Words

```
P P U R P L E B E A C H
L R G A P P Z D F V N K
I J I O T M O F B O H N
V R D N U H C T O O S P
I F W R C U A T A W U U
N O H C P E A B N S O L
G S E R S K A X A T H M
S S A W S W D L I S Z V
K I T A H A J N B L C B
I L S I K C A Z Y E T A
E S K N I M O F N A R K
S Z X L F R E G I N A T
```

Things to Know About Saskatchewan

- Saskatchewan is one of two landlocked provinces
- It is the world's largest producer of potash, used in fertilizer
- The province grows more than 50 percent of Canada's wheat
- Curling is the official sport
- There are two national parks – Prince Albert National Park and Grasslands National Park
- Lake Athabasca is the largest lake in the province at almost 8,000 square kilometers
- There are many purple sand beaches in Saskatchewan
- The most popular food in Saskatchewan is Saskatoon Berry Pie
- Saskatchewan gets the most sunshine of all the Canadian provinces
- The province is nicknamed the Land of the Living Skies

- The population density in the province is only 2 people per square kilometer
- Saskatchewans love hockey, the province produces the most National Hockey League players per capita
- There are over 100,000 lakes in the province

Color the Flag!

- Little Lake Manitou is known as the Dead Sea of Canada, it has such a high mineral content that you cannot sink in its waters
- Saskatchewan averages 12-18 tornadoes per year
- The largest T-Rex fossil ever discovered was found here

Yukon

Motto: *None*

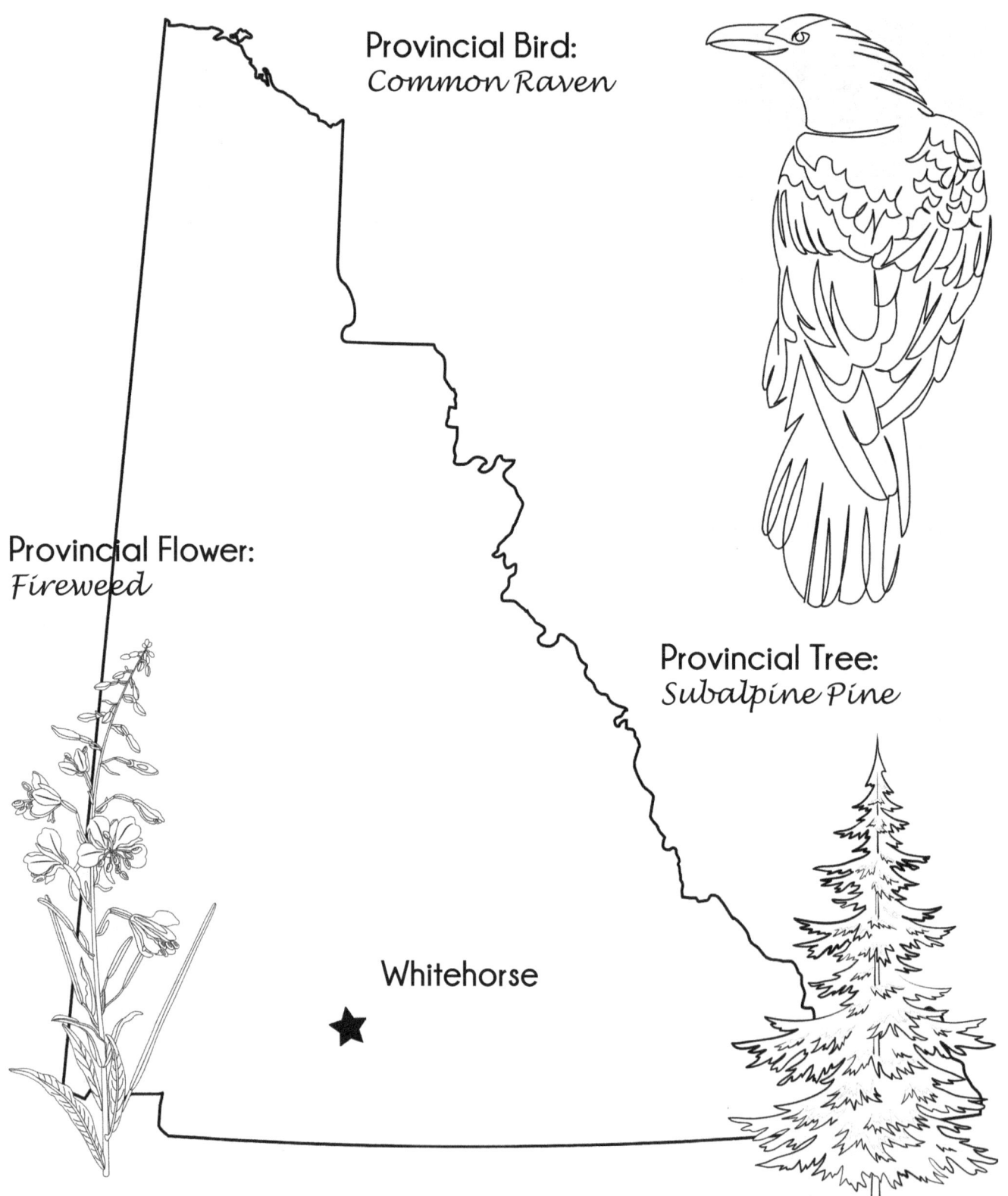

Provincial Bird: *Common Raven*

Provincial Flower: *Fireweed*

Provincial Tree: *Subalpine Pine*

Whitehorse

Facts About Yukon

Capital: Whitehorse

Confederation: June 13, 1998

Language(s): English, French

Postal Abbreviation: YT

Major Cities: Whitehorse

Population: 40,232

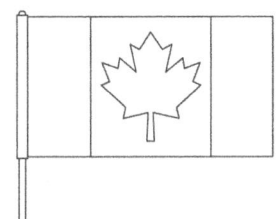

CARIBOU
DOG SLED
FIREWEED
ICEFIELDS
MIGRATION
MINING
MOUNT LOGAN
VUNTUT
WHITEHORSE
YUKON

Find the Words

```
M F Y L Q C A R I B O U
O I E U Y M R C W M P M
U R Y I K M I N I N G V
N E M Z B O S I V Z P I
T W J W B G N C T B M Z
L E W H I T E H O R S E
O E I C E F I E L D S V
G D A J H S F D B Q L U
A M I G R A T I O N H N
N J G L Y F L C Y Y O T
A G I N K T I M B B X U
G D O G S L E D S Q P T
```

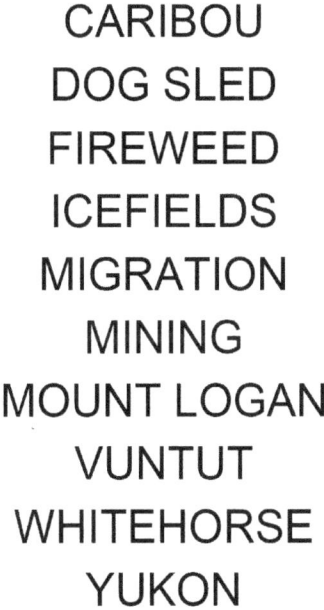

Things to Know About Yukon

- Yukon is the smallest territory in Canada at 482,433 square kilometers (186,272 square miles), but it is larger than four of the provinces
- Mount Logan (5959 meters) is the highest peak in Canada and the second-highest in North America; it is also the world's largest non-volcanic mountain
- St. Elias Icefields is the world's largest non-polar icefield and contains over 2,000 glaciers
- It is also home to the world's smallest desert; Carcross Desert is only 2.6 square kilometers
- The territory was named after the Yukon River, which is the second-longest river in Canada; the name means "great river"
- The Yukon is the westernmost point in Canada
- Every year 200,000 porcupine caribou embark on the world's longest mammal migration in Yukon
- Whitehorse (population 28,000) is the only city in the Yukon
- Yukon is nicknamed The Land of the Midnight Sun because the sun does not set in the peak of winter
- Snag, Yukon has the lowest temperature ever recorded in Canada at -63 degrees Celsius (-81F) on February 3, 1947
- There are three national parks in Yukon – Kluane, Vuntut, and Ivvavik national parks
- The Yukon Quest dog sled race is a 1600 km

Color the Flag!

(1,000 mile) race from Whitehorse to Fairbanks, Alaska
- One of the best places in the world to see the Northern Lights is the Yukon
- Mining is the territory's most important industry, followed by tourism
- The books *Call of the Wild* and *White Fang* by Jack London are set in the Yukon during the Klondike Gold Rush
- The Bering Land Bridge, which was used by prehistoric peoples to cross from Asia into North America is in parts of central and northern Yukon

Capitals

Match the letter of the correct capital for the provinces, territories, and nation.

1. Alberta _____
2. British Columbia _____
3. Canada _____
4. Manitoba _____
5. New Brunswick _____
6. Newfoundland and Labrador _____
7. Northwest Territories _____
8. Nova Scotia _____
9. Nunavut _____
10. Ontario _____
11. Prince Edward Island _____
12. Quebec _____
13. Saskatchewan _____
14. Yukon _____

---

a. Charlottetown b. Edmonton c. Fredericton d. Halifax e. Iqaluit f. Ottawa g. Quebec City h. Regina i. St. John's j. Toronto k. Victoria l. Whitehorse m. Winnipeg n. Yellowknife

Label the Map

Test your knowledge! Fill in the names of the provinces and territories.

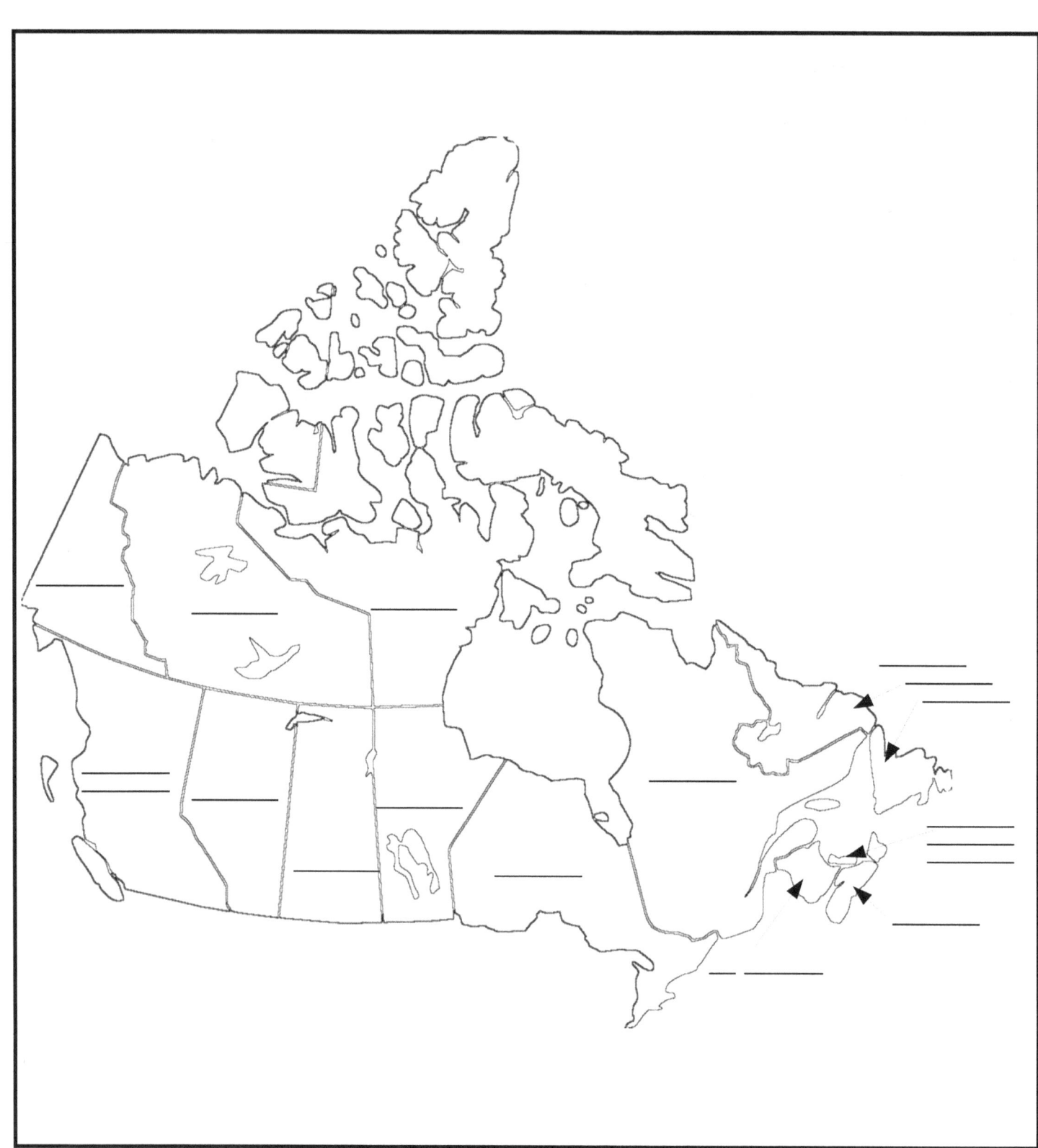

Canada Crossword

Across

1. Provincial tree of Manitoba (5,6)
9. Whitehorse is the capital (5)
10. Bay of Fundy has the highest _____ in the world (5)
11. The capital of British Columbia (8)
14. Northwest Territories is also known as the land of the _____ (8,3)
16. Halifax is the capital (4,6)
17. Capital of New Brunswick (11)
19. A national park in Alberta (5)
21. Largest lake entirely within Canada (5,4)
22. Niagara Falls are in this province (7)
23. Majority French-speaking province (6)
24. The number of national parks in British Columbia (5)
25. Country that borders Canada (6,6)

Down

2. Most populated city in Canada (7)
3. Animal that embarks on longest mammal migration in Yukon (7)
4. Newfoundland and Labrador were first to respond to distress signal from this ship (7)
5. Capital of Saskatchewan (6)
6. Place that is home to many covered bridges (3,9)
7. A large whirlpool in New Brunswick (3,3)
8. The westernmost province (7,8)
9. Capital of Northwest Territories (11)
12. Bridge that links New Brunswick and Prince Edward island (13)
13. The provincial bird of Newfoundland and Labrador (6)
14. Winnipeg is its capital (8)
15. One of two landlocked provinces (7)
18. Provincial fish of Saskatchewan (7)
20. Largest province by area (7)

Color the Flag

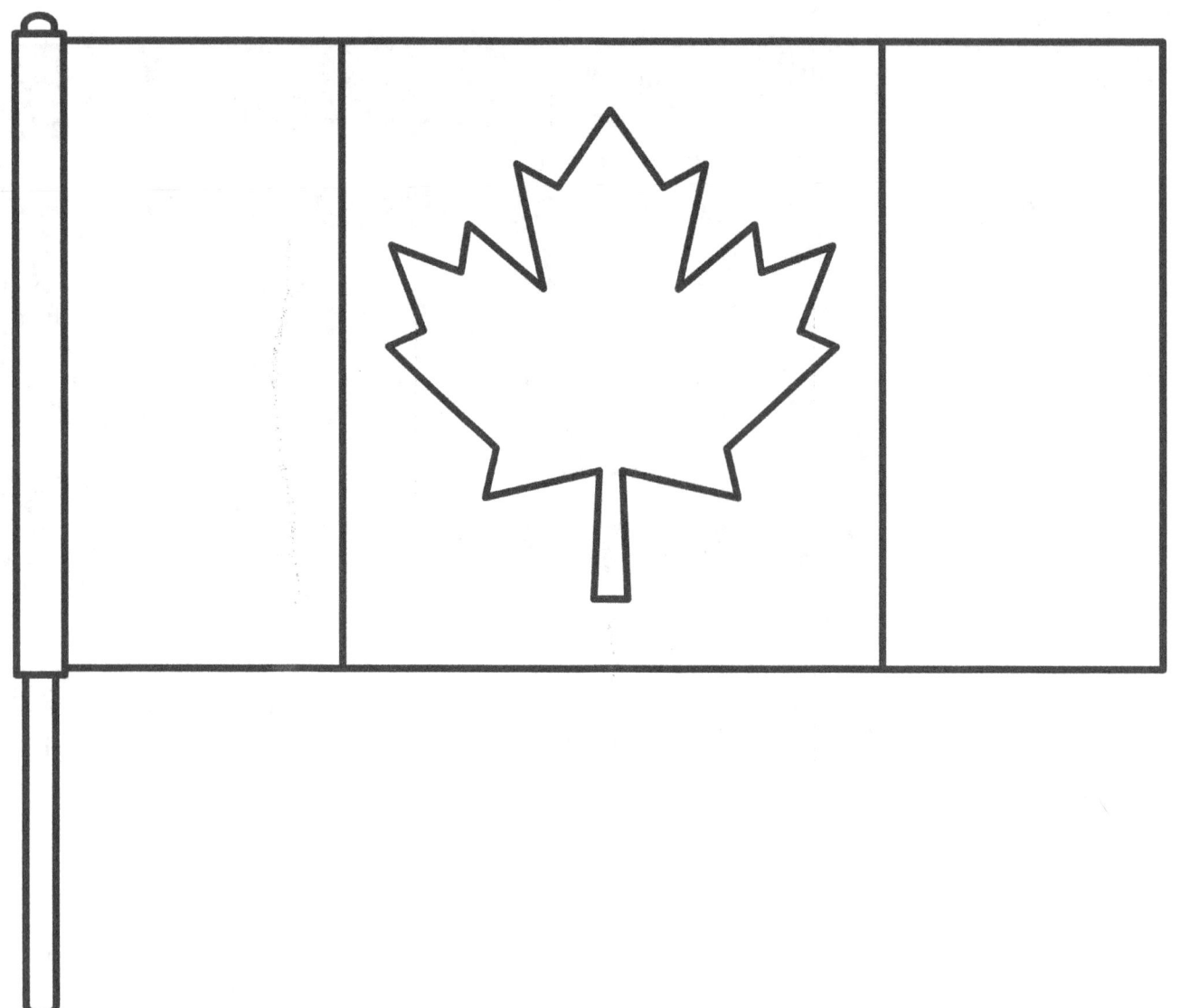

The Canadian National Flag consists of two red rectangles on each side of a white square with a red maple leaf in the center. Red and white are the official colors of Canada. The 11-point red maple leaf is the national emblem of Canada and was designed by Jacques Saint-Cyr. The current flag design was adopted in 1965 and replaced the British flag as the National Flag of Canada.

Answers

1. Alberta and Saskatchewan
2. Nunavut
3. Ontario
4. British Columbia
5. British Columbia, Saskatchewan, Northwest Territories
6. Prince Edward Island
7. Newfoundland and Labrador
8. British Columbia, Alberta, Saskatchewan, Manitoba, Ontario, Quebec, New Brunswick, Yukon

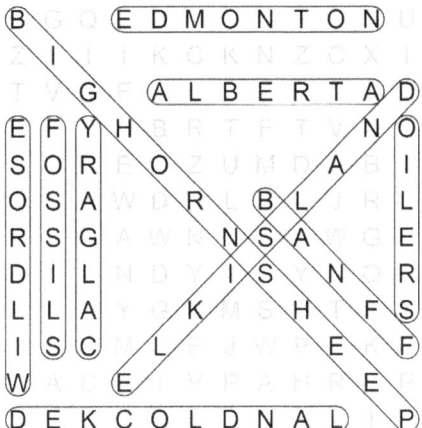

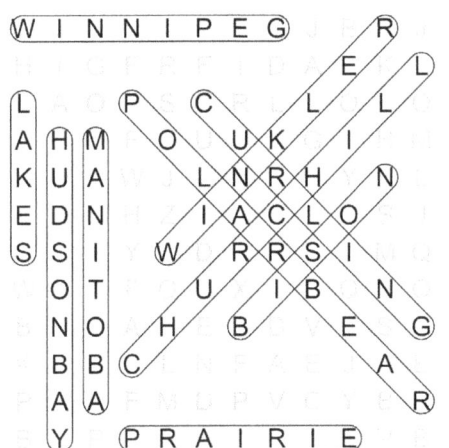

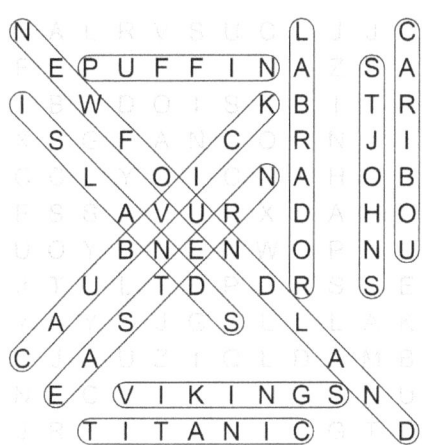

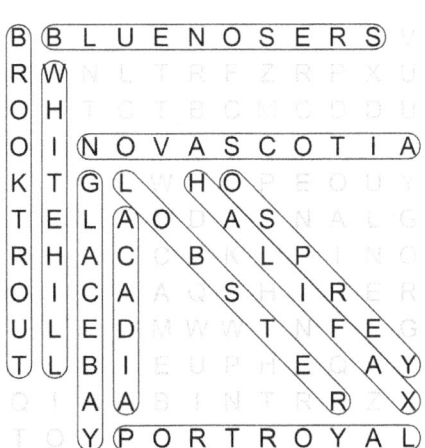
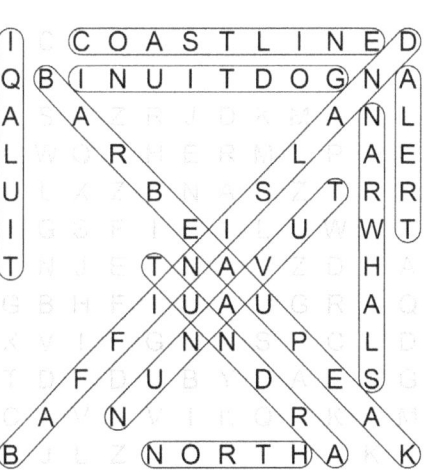

Answers

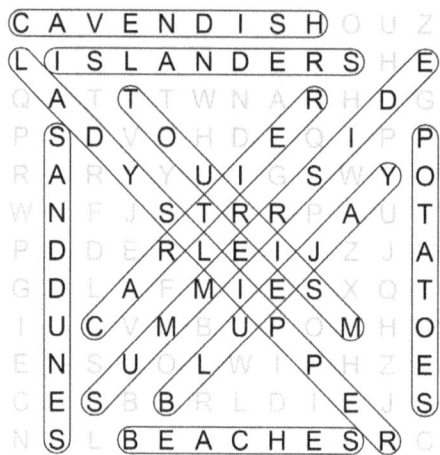

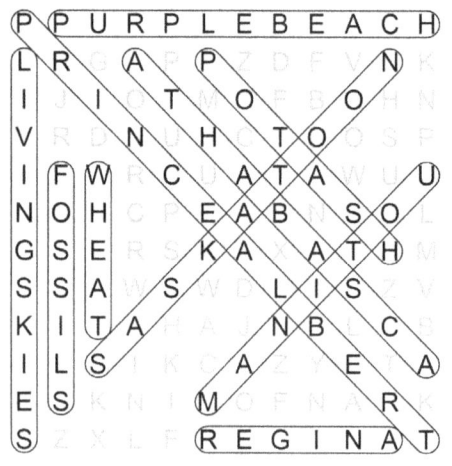
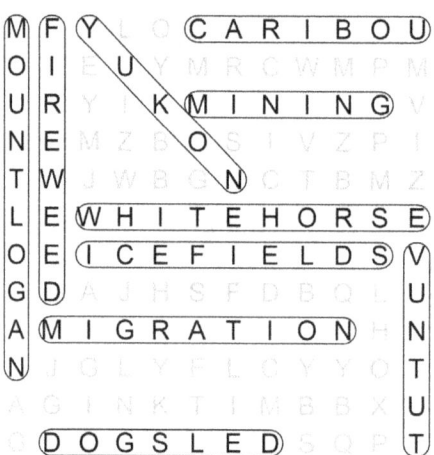

1. b
2. k
3. f
4. m
5. c
6. i
7. n
8. d
9. e
10. j
11. a
12. g
13. h
14. l